Your Perfect Right

Your Perfect Right

Eighth Edition

ASSERTIVENESS
and **EQUALITY** in Your
LIFE and **RELATIONSHIPS**

Robert **Alberti**   Michael **Emmons**

Impact **Publishers,** Inc.
ATASCADERO, CALIFORNIA

Editions
First Edition, October, 1970; Second Edition, January, 1974;
Third Edition, May, 1978; Fouth Edition, April 1982;
Fifth Edition, July, 1986; Sixth Edition, October, 1990; Seventh Edition, October 1995;
Eighth Edition, April 2001
Copyright © 1970, 1974, 1978, 1982, 1986, 1990, 1995, 2001
by Robert E. Alberti and Michael L. Emmons
Fourth Printing, July 2006

ATTENTION ORGANIZATIONS AND CORPORATIONS:
This book is available at quantity discounts on bulk purchases for educational,
business, or sales promotional use. For further information, please contact Impact
Publishers, P.O. Box 6016, Atascadero, CA 93423-6016, Phone: 1-800-246-7228,
e-mail: sales@impactpublishers.com

Library of Congress Cataloging-in-Publication Data

Alberti, Robert E.
    Your perfect right : assertiveness and equality in your life and
relationships/ Robert Alberti, Michael Emmons.-- 8th ed.
        p. cm.
    Includes bibliographical references and index.
    ISBN 1-886230-36-6 (cloth) -- ISBN 1-886230-28-5 (paper)
        1. Assertiveness (Psychology) 2. Interpersonal communication.
    I. Emmons, Michael L. II. Title.

RC489.A77 A53 2001
158.2--dc21   2001024152

Publisher's Note
*This publication is designed to provide accurate and authoritative information in regard to the
subject matter covered. It is sold with the understanding that the publisher is not engaged in
rendering psychological, medical, or other professional services. If expert assistance or
counseling is needed, the services of a competent professional should be sought.*

Impact Publishers and colophon are registered trademarks of Impact Publishers, Inc.

Cover design by George Foster, Foster & Foster, Inc. Fairfield, Iowa
Printed in the United States of America on acid-free paper,
Published by *Impact ✲ Publishers, Inc.*
POST OFFICE BOX 6016
ATASCADERO, CALIFORNIA 93423-6016
www.impactpublishers.com

Contents

PART IV: APPLYING YOUR ASSERTIVENESS

PART V: LIVING AN ASSERTIVE LIFE

APPENDICES

Acknowledgements

We're as humbled as we are honored that so many readers, reviewers, therapists, and others have found value in these pages over the last three decades. Eight editions, a million-and-a-quarter copies in print, lots of glowing feedback . . . it's very rewarding to know our work may have touched so many lives.

And, of course, we didn't accomplish this alone. Hundreds — perhaps thousands — of colleagues, known and unknown, in psychology and the other human service professions have recognized this book with their honest critiques, support, praise, and recommendation to clients. We are very grateful to know that you consider this the best of the many books on the subject of assertiveness, and one of the best of all self-help books. (Blush.) We hope this eighth edition will continue to serve as a valuable resource to your clients.

Many, many people have contributed to our knowledge and to the success of *Your Perfect Right* over the last three decades. As we attempt to thank those who have made direct contributions, we're bound to miss a few. Please accept our apologies if you're not mentioned here. It's not because we don't appreciate your help; it's because we're not perfect. Special thanks go to Judy Appelbaum, Nancy Austin, Albert Ellis, Kay Emmons, Cyril Franks, Carol Geer, W. Harold Grant, Chuck Hillinger, Arnold Lazarus, Lachlan MacDonald, Carita and Charles Merker (deceased), Stanlee Phelps, all our friends at Research Press (in part because they didn't publish it), Mike Serber (deceased), Janet Wolfe, Joseph Wolpe (deceased), and the dedicated staff at Impact Publishers over the years.

Finally, Bob wants to add a very special recognition to Deborah Alberti, for over four decades of support and loving partnership.

R.E.A.
M.L.E.

Atascadero and San Luis Obispo, California
February 2001

Part I

You and Your Perfect Right

Assertiveness and You

*Be fair with others,
but then keep after them
until they're fair with you.*
— ALAN ALDA

AITLIN LOOKED AT HER WATCH — 7:15. Sean would be furious, or worried sick, she knew. Her boss had appeared at Caitlin's desk at 4:55 and asked her to get this report ready for the Board meeting at 8:15 in the morning. It wasn't the first time . . .

Anger, confusion, even helplessness are feelings that can result from situations like these. What can you do? How can you express your feelings when such frustrations come up? There are no easy answers, but there are answers, if you are willing to make the effort. It may require that you make some changes in your life.

Changing yourself is challenging, and not easy, but you can do it, and we'll show you how. This book offers you a proven step-by-step method — assertiveness training — for improving your relationships with others. If you'll follow it, we're confident it can work for you. Millions of folks have learned to express themselves more effectively and achieve more of their life goals using these procedures.

If you're looking for lessons in how to manipulate others, you're reading the wrong book. We believe there's too much of that in the world already. We advocate assertiveness as a tool for making your relationships more equal — for avoiding the one-down feeling that often comes when you fail to express what you really want.

The process itself is fairly simple. We'll teach you some basic principles, give you some examples, and present a series of specific procedures for you to follow. Your job — if you decide to try this approach — is to read carefully and carry out the steps we've outlined.

Sound like a lot of work? Not really. It just takes persistence, and a determination to make your life better!

Who Needs It?

Jeanette was really upset when her neighbor came over and talked nonstop for forty-five minutes about neighborhood gossip. Mostly, she was upset with herself for letting it happen . . . again.

Is this stuff mainly for those — like Jeanette — who aren't able to stand up for themselves? Only partly. We wrote the first edition of this book (in 1970) for folks who have that trouble, but we've learned a lot over the years, and one thing we now know is that *everyone* needs a hand at times in getting along better with others.

If you're like most of us, your personal power is diminished every day — at home, on the job, at school, in stores and restaurants, in club meetings — in ways both trivial and important. Many people find themselves at a loss for just the right action.

How do you handle it when . . .

. . . you want to cut short a telephone sales pitch?

. . . a co-worker puts you down?

. . . your spouse gives you a dirty look?

. . . a neighbor blasts his stereo until 3 A.M.?

. . . one of your children snaps at you?

Are you able to express warm, positive feelings to another person? Are you comfortable starting a conversation with strangers at a party? Do you sometimes feel ineffective in making your
✳ desires clear to others? Do you have difficulty saying "no" to

persuasive people? Are you often at the bottom of the "pecking order," pushed around by others? Or maybe you're the one who pushes others around to get your way?

> *Assertiveness is a tool for making your relationships more equal.*

At times like these we all need "survival tactics" — ways to respond that let others know something's wrong. Some folks swallow their feelings, say nothing, and remain upset. Others blast the offender with a punishing, put-down response.

We think there's a better way. We advocate *equality* as a style. Not "getting your way." Not "getting back at" the other person. And not "turning the other cheek." We think the important thing is to *affirm self-worth* — both yours and the other person's. *Key*

Although there's no one "right way" to handle such events, there are some basic principles which will help you to gain confidence and effectiveness in your relationships with others. You're going to learn those principles as you read this book. You'll discover how to develop and use tactics that are fair, leaving both parties with their self-respect intact. ☺

You don't have to intimidate others in order to avoid being intimidated. And you don't have to allow yourself to be pushed around by anybody. By learning to be effectively *assertive*, you can deal with such upsets directly and honestly, and keep everyone on an equal footing — most of the time, anyway.

THE ASSERTIVE ALTERNATIVE

Travis and Linda were not sure if the waiter had forgotten them, was ignoring them, or was simply very busy. He had not been at their table for at least fifteen minutes. And they had theater tickets . . .

Assertiveness is an alternative to personal powerlessness or manipulation. You'll find in this book a program which will help you develop effective ways to express yourself, maintain your self-respect, *and* show respect for others. We firmly believe in the equal worth of every human being, and this book celebrates that belief, and encourages positive relationships between persons who respect and value each other.

There are lots of popular ideas you may have heard about what it means to be assertive. Unfortunately, we don't agree with most of them! An old "Ziggy" cartoon, for example, illustrates the unfortunate image that many hold. We find our hero walking up to a door labeled "Assertiveness Training Class." Below that sign is another: "Don't Bother to Knock, Barge Right In!" (You can probably guess our view: *barging in is not being assertive!*)——

Some popular books talk about "assertiveness" as a technique for getting your way. That's not our goal. As we've said, you won't find gimmicks on how to manipulate others in this book. We advocate a less aggressive view of self-expression, and have tried to correct that false concept of assertiveness. We'll help you to clarify your personal goals in relationships, and we'll show you how to retain a sense of control, a sense of power in your own life, without trying to control others in the process.

Aggression and assertion are commonly confused, but assertive behavior doesn't push others around, deny their rights, or run roughshod over them. Assertiveness reflects genuine concern for everybody's rights. *clue*

Here's our definition of healthy assertive action:

> *Assertive behavior promotes equality in human relationships, enabling us to act in our own best interests, to stand up for ourselves without undue anxiety, to express honest feelings comfortably, to exercise personal rights without denying the rights of others.*

Confronted with a difficult situation, lots of folks tend to respond nonassertively, thinking of an appropriate comeback long after the opportunity has passed. Others react aggressively, and make a deep and negative impression that they often regret later. By developing a more adequate repertoire of assertive behavior, you may choose appropriate and self-fulfilling responses in a variety of situations.

BARRIERS TO SELF-EXPRESSION

In helping thousands of persons learn to value themselves and to express themselves directly and honestly, we have found three particularly difficult barriers to self-assertion:

- ❖ Many people don't *believe they have the right* to be assertive;
- ❖ Many people are highly *anxious or fearful* about being assertive;
- ❖ Many people lack the *skills* to express themselves effectively.

In this book we've addressed these barriers to personal power and healthy relationships, and have given you proven, effective tools to overcome them.

In later chapters, the concepts of *nonassertive, aggressive, assertive* behavior are illustrated with lots of examples and specific instructions. And we've tried to avoid the "psychobabble" that often makes its way into self-help books!

(In a separate manual for professionals, *Assertiveness and Social Skills Training*, we have expanded on the theoretical and procedural aspects of facilitating assertive behavior in others, as a guide for therapists.)

HOW CAN YOU BENEFIT FROM THIS BOOK?

Learning to make assertive responses will reduce the anxiety you may feel in dealing with others. Even such physical complaints as headaches, general fatigue, stomach disturbances, rashes, and asthma may be related to a failure to develop assertive behavior. *wow*

Assertiveness can help you avoid such symptoms. Research has shown that, by developing the ability to stand up for yourself and do things on your own initiative, you can cut down your stress and increase your sense of worth as a person. You can be healthier, more in charge of yourself in relationships, more confident and capable, more spontaneous in expressing your feelings. And you'll likely find yourself more admired by others as well. *benefit*

Whether your goals are personal, social, job-related, or world-changing, you will find a careful reading-and-practice approach

You won't find gimmicks on how to manipulate others in this book.

to these ideas and procedures will help you to develop more effective self-expression and healthier relationships.

Hundreds of research studies have proved the value of assertiveness training, and countless thousands of individuals who had trouble expressing their feelings have achieved greater self-fulfillment by following this program. We believe you can find similar help here. We are especially pleased that thousands of therapists have recommended the book as helpful reading for their clients. In three separate surveys of practicing professionals, this book has consistently received the highest rating among assertiveness books, and has been among the most-often recommended of all self-help books.

Before you go on to the next chapter, think a bit about your own goals. Why did you pick up this book? Are you looking for help in specific areas of your life — on the job perhaps, or with your family relationships? In what ways would you like your life to be different? Chapter 8 goes into specifics about setting goals for your growth, but give a few moments thought now to what you'd like to gain from reading *Your Perfect Right*. Then, when you're ready, push ahead and let's find out what this "assertiveness" stuff is all about.

So as to cut down on my stress; I want to beable to increase my sense of worth as a person, to be more confident + capable, spontenous in recognizing my own feelings + expressing them to others in a respectful way to both parties.

2

Whose Perfect Right?

Between people, as among nations,
respect of each other's rights
insures the peace.
— BENITO JUAREZ

EVERY INDIVIDUAL has the same fundamental human rights as every other, regardless of gender, age, ethnicity, role or title.

If that notion is not idealistic enough for you, here's another: we'd like to see everyone exercise their rights without infringing on the rights of others. Equality is fundamental to assertive living. The *Universal Declaration of Human Rights*, adopted by the United Nations General Assembly in 1948, is an excellent statement of goals for human relationships. It too is idealistic, and we doubt that any country in the world lives up to its ideals entirely. Still, we urge you to let those principles encourage you to support the rights of every individual — including yourself!

As we embark upon the twenty-first century and second millennium, we can hail progress around the globe toward the development of societies based upon these values. Individuals and groups have spoken out, and some intolerable conditions have changed. It appears that relationships, from the most intimate of love partners to the most distant of neighbors and co-workers, have begun to reflect a more equal valuing of both persons. Assertiveness training has had something to do with some of those needed changes, and we're proud to acknowledge that this book, first published in 1970, has been a contributor to that process.

Keeping a broad view of individual human rights can help us to counteract the forces that pit us against one another. We are all human beings after all, citizens of a very small planet, and dependent upon each other in many ways. We need mutual support and understanding for our very survival.

ARE SOME MORE EQUAL THAN OTHERS?
Unfortunately, society often evaluates human beings on scales which rank some people as more important than others. Here are a few popular notions about the value of persons. Which ones do you agree with?

Adults are more important than children

Bosses are more important than employees

Men are more important than women

Whites are more important than people of color

Physicians are more important than plumbers

Teachers are more important than students

Politicians are more important than voters

Generals are more important than privates

Winners are more important than losers

Americans are more important than "foreigners"

The list could go on and on. Many of our society's organizations tend to perpetuate these myths, and to allow individuals in these roles to be treated as if they were of lesser value as human beings. The good news, however, is that lots of folks are finding ways to express themselves as equals.

honesty!

ASSERTIVE WOMEN IN THE TWENTY-FIRST CENTURY

In their excellent book, *The Assertive Woman,* Stanlee Phelps and Nancy Austin present the behavioral styles of four "women we all know." Their characterizations of *Doris Doormat, Agatha Aggressive, Iris Indirect,* and *April Assertive,* are self-explanatory by the names alone. Yet, in describing the patterns of each, Phelps and Austin help us to gain a clearer picture of the social mores which have devalued assertiveness in women. Agatha gets her way, though she hasn't many friends. Iris, the sly one, also gains most of what she wants, and sometimes her "victims" never even know it. Doris, although denied her own wishes much of the time, is highly praised by men and by the power structure as "a good woman." April's honesty and forthrightness have often led her into trouble (at least until recently) at home, at school, on the job, and even with other women.

The assertive woman is valued by society, by men, by other women. She is capable of choosing her own lifestyle, free of dictates of tradition, government, husband, children, social groups, bosses. She may elect to be a homemaker and not fear intimidation by her "liberated" sisters. She may elect to pursue a male-dominated profession and enjoy confidence in her rights and abilities.

In her sexual relationships an assertive woman can be comfortable taking initiative, asking for what she wants (and thereby freeing her partner from the expected role of making the first move). She and her partner can share equally in the expression of intimacy.

She can say "no" with firmness — and can make it stick — to requests for favors, to unwanted sexual advances, to her family's expectations that she "do it all."

As a consumer, she can make the marketplace respond to her needs by refusing to accept shoddy merchandise, service, or marketing techniques.

In short, the assertive *woman* is an assertive *person* who exhibits the qualities we espouse throughout this book; and she likes herself — and is liked — better for it!

aggressive: marked by combative readiness, driving energy, more intensive argumentative, belligerent, contentious

doormat: mat to wipe feet on

indirect: not straight / not straight forward & open, not directly to the point / long winded, deceitful, dishonest, insidious, misleading

By developing the ability to stand up for yourself and do things on your own initiative, you can cut down your stress and increase your sense of worth as a person.

A number of factors combined to help women achieve long overdue gains in recognition of their individual rights. The popularity of assertiveness training for women, including specialized workshops in management and other fields, is one hopeful sign. Women of all social viewpoints, ethnic and socio-economic backgrounds, educational and professional involvements — homemakers, hard hats, and high ranking executives — have made phenomenal gains in assertive expression.

help

Society has recognized the inadequacy of an "ideal" which identifies women as characteristically "passive, sweet, and submissive." At long last, the assertive woman is valued.

What's more, some of these changes are being felt worldwide. This book and *The Assertive Woman* have been translated and published in China, Germany, Israel, Japan and many other countries. Press reports indicate that women in some Muslim societies are beginning to openly seek personal and political equality. In Japan, a survey reported in 1990 by a major bank showed that 28 percent of employees would welcome a female boss; the figure a decade earlier had been 12 percent. And local governments in Japan have offered classes in business expertise for women entrepreneurs.

MEN CAN BE ASSERTIVE TOO!

Imagine the following scene: John's day has been exhausting; he has washed windows, mopped floors, completed three loads of wash, and continuously picked up and cleaned up after the children. He is now working hurriedly in the kitchen preparing for dinner. The children are running in and out of the house banging the door, screaming, throwing toys.

In the midst of this chaos, Mary arrives home from an equally trying day at her office. She offers a cursory "I'm home!" as she

Cursory:

passes the kitchen on her way to the family room. Dropping her briefcase and kicking off her shoes, she flops in her favorite chair in front of the television set, calling out, "John, bring me a beer! I've had a helluva day!"

This scene is humorous, partly because it is non-traditional. After all, shouldn't John also have a career, working for a salary instead of at home? Isn't a man's place to go out and conquer the world on behalf of his family? To demonstrate his manhood, his macho, his strength and courage?

For too long we accepted as proper the stereotype of the male as "mighty hunter," who must protect and provide for his family. Indeed, from earliest childhood, the accepted male roles of earlier days encouraged assertive — and often aggressive — behavior in pursuit of this "ideal." Competitiveness, achievement, striving to be the best were integral components of male child-rearing and formal schooling — much more so than for their sisters. Men have been treated as if they were by nature strong, active, decisive, dominant, cool, rational.

Late in the twentieth century, a growing number of men began to acknowledge a great gap in their preparation for interpersonal relationships. Limited in the past to only two options — the powerful, dominating aggressor or the wimp with sand in his face — most found neither to be particularly satisfying. Assertiveness offered them an effective alternative, and a new generation of men have rejected the aggressive, climbing, "success" stereotype in favor of a more balanced role and lifestyle.

Psychological concepts of "masculinity" have changed to acknowledge the caring, nurturing side of men as well. Men have recognized that they can accomplish their own life goals in assertive — not aggressive — ways. Professional advancement is available for the competent, confident, assertive man.

We have witnessed remarkable changes in our society's definition of what it means to be a man. The emerging definition looks remarkably like the *assertive man* we have been advocating for over three decades: firm but not pushy, self-confident but not arrogant) self-assertive but committed to equality in relationships, open and direct but (not) dominant.

"Traditional" male activities continue to reflect the old ways, of course, but a growing number of men are moving beyond sports teams, adult "fraternities" and community service clubs to form personal growth and consciousness-raising groups (not unlike those their wives, sisters and mothers formed decades before). "Male bonding," although still material for stand-up comic routines and sit-com segments, is no longer a joke for tens of thousands of men who are seeking something more meaningful than a weekly backslapping lunch with the Old Boys Club.

We admire those men who are beginning to acknowledge to themselves and to each other (if not yet to women), their needs and desires, their strengths and their vulnerabilities, their anxieties and their guilt, the internal and external pressures that drive their lives.

Assertive men are held in high esteem in relationships with the important others in their lives. Family and friends are closer to and have greater respect for the man who is comfortable enough with himself that he needn't put others down in order to put himself up. The honesty of assertiveness is an incalculable asset in close personal relationships, and assertive men are coming to value such closeness right along with the traditional rewards of economic success.

Researchers who have studied large groups of men over long time periods have noted that many men who lived the aggressive style in their 20s and 30s found that those achievements meant little in their later years. The values of personal intimacy, family closeness, and trusted friendships — all fostered by assertiveness, openness, honesty — are the lasting and important ones.

The assertive man is finding himself too!

LIVING IN A MULTICULTURAL, PLURALISTIC WORLD

The essence of our approach to assertiveness training has always been *equality*. The goal of this book is to foster better communication between equals, not to help one to be superior over another or to step on others to get her way. Open and honest communication — mutual, cooperative, affirming — is the process which can achieve the desired outcome of equality — a place for everyone.

These days, however, that goal may be more challenging than ever before, as the world grows smaller. Global economic, political, and personal changes have led to more awareness of and direct contact with people of different cultural backgrounds. Every day, right here at home, most of us can see that the world is becoming a multicultural "mixing pot" to a greater degree than ever before. It's exciting and refreshing to see different faces and hear different languages and encounter different lifestyles.

At times, it can also be uncomfortable.

No other nation has the cultural diversity of the United States. Our home state of California is in the forefront of the interface of cultures. In fact, whites are now a minority in California. More than half of the population of the Golden State are people of color: Hispanic/Latino, African American, Asian, Native American, and other ethnic groups. In the public schools — a microcosm of the larger society — teachers of English as a second language face a sea of faces from dozens of diverse cultures. In one Los Angeles school, a reported 22 different languages are spoken!

As California's multi-ethnic population has grown, similar population changes will occur throughout the United States in the decades to come.

Can we all live together? Do we respect and value one another? Or are we threatened by the entry of each newcomer, each "foreigner," each person who is "different"?

Protection of human rights, equality of treatment, respect for persons regardless of ethnic or personal traits — the more we can become aware of, and understand and accept each other — including those who are "different" — the stronger we will be as individuals (and as a nation and world).

HOW DIFFERENT IS "DIFFERENT"?

When people think about other cultures, it is commonly assumed that "all people from a culture behave in the same way." For too long, argues UCLA professor Steven Lopez, "understanding" people of other backgrounds has meant lumping cultural groups together and ignoring individuals. Such stereotyping *creates* barriers, it doesn't erase them.

You hear, as we hear, stereotypes about other cultures all the time. Here are a few: in some cultures if a woman smiles at a stranger it has sexual implications; African American males do not like to maintain eye contact in conversations; the male rules the household in the Mexican American culture; Saudi Arabians stand very close and seldom use their right hand when communicating; in some cultures the death of a loved one is a joyous occasion.

Can it be that all people from a certain culture (or all women, or all teenagers) have the same beliefs? Or act the same way? Of course not. And such stereotypic assumptions are as dangerous as they are false. We get into trouble when we assume that all people from any group behave in the same way or share the same beliefs.

The catch is that it's equally false — and dangerous — to assume that "people are people" and deep down we're all alike as human beings, regardless of our groups. Culture, gender, age *are* important, and to understand an individual requires that you acknowledge these vital characteristics. And treat them *individually*.

Facial expression of emotions, for example, is more-or-less universal for humans everywhere, but cultural customs as well as personal genetic and biochemical makeup determine whether or not and when an individual's face will show anger or joy or fear or grief. Interpreting such a complex component of behavior is not simple!

How True

Culture, genders, age.

What Does Background Have to Do With Assertiveness?

As you begin to develop growing assertive skills, how can you use them in dealing with people from different backgrounds? First, treat each person with respect; second, educate yourself about the backgrounds of people you encounter; and third, if something seems unusual in an individual's style — standing too close, avoiding eye contact, being overly shy or pushy — check it out. You might say something such as, ("I've noticed that you stand very close to me when we talk. I'm not used to that. Can you tell me what that's about?")

Keep in mind that each human being is unique, a complex blend of age, gender, genes, culture, beliefs and personal life experiences. All Italians, or Irish, or Vietnamese, or Mexicans are not alike, but members of each group have much in common. All teenagers, or senior citizens, or pre-schoolers are not the same, but it helps to know something about the needs and characteristics of his group as you deal with an individual. All working women, or midlife men, or "thirtysomethings" are not identical, but they have similarities that *may* be important to know if you want to get to know someone who fits one of those labels.

In sum, as you seek to understand people of other cultures or backgrounds, *begin first with the individual.* Don't underestimate cultural or group-specific behavior or overestimate the universality of human behavior. When in doubt, show respect, ask questions and listen, listen, listen.

Society Often Discourages Assertiveness

Despite important improvements in some areas, society's rewards for appropriate assertive behavior are still limited. The assertions of each individual, the right of self-expression without fear or guilt, the right to a dissenting opinion, and the unique contribution of each person — all need greater recognition. We can't over-emphasize the importance of the difference between appropriate *assertion* and the destructive *aggression* with which it is often confused.

> *Each of us has the right to be and to express ourselves, and to feel good (not powerless or guilty) about doing so, as long as we do not hurt others in the process.*

Assertion is often actively discouraged, in subtle — or not so subtle — ways in the family, at school, at work, in church, in our political institutions, and elsewhere.

In the *family*, the child who decides to speak up for his or her rights is often promptly censored: "Don't talk to your mother (father) that way!" "Children are to be seen, not heard." "Don't be disrespectful!" "Never let me hear you talk like that again!" Obviously, these common parental commands are not conducive to a child's assertion of self!

At *school*, teachers are frequently inhibitors of assertion. Quiet, well-behaved children who do not question authority are rewarded, whereas those who "buck the system" in some way are dealt with sternly. Educators acknowledge that the child's natural spontaneity in learning is conditioned out no later than the fourth or fifth grade, replaced by conformity to the school's approach.

The results of such upbringing affect functioning on the job, and the *workplace* itself often is no help. At work, employees are aware that it's best not to do or say anything that will rock the boat. The boss is in charge, and everyone else is expected to "go along with the program" — even if they consider the expectations completely inappropriate. Early work experiences in the past taught that those who speak up are not likely to obtain raises or recognition, and may even lose their jobs. You quickly learn not to make waves, to keep things running smoothly, to have few ideas of your own, to be careful how you act lest it get back to the boss.

Fortunately, things have changed somewhat in recent years, with greater employee rights and a better balance emerging. A collegial atmosphere now pervades high-tech firms. Low unemployment has required employers to accommodate a variety of individuals with talent. Many people work at home, as independent contractors or telecommuting for virtually all of their working lives. The fear of speaking out on the job is not so widespread as it once was, but there are still many subtle influences that suggest it's best to be nonassertive at work!

The teachings of many *churches* suggest that assertive behavior is somehow at odds with religious commitment. Such qualities as humility, self-denial, and self-sacrifice may be encouraged, to the exclusion of standing up for oneself. There is a mistaken notion that religious ideals must, in some mystical way, be incompatible with feeling good about oneself and with being calm and confident in relationships with others. Quite the contrary; assertiveness is not only compatible with the teachings of major religions, it frees you of self-defeating behavior, allowing you to be of greater service to others as well as to yourself!

Political institutions are not so likely as the home, school and church to influence early development of assertive behavior, but they do little to encourage its expression. Political decision-making remains largely inaccessible to the average citizen. Nevertheless, it is still true that the "squeaking wheel gets greased," and when individuals –- especially when they get together in groups — become expressive enough, governments usually respond.

We have been gratified to see assertive expression succeed — without aggression —among the activist politically alienated. The growth and successes of assertive citizen lobbies — minority/ homeless/children's/gay and other rights movements, Common Cause (for political reform), AARP and Grey Panthers (for older Americans), the various tax reform movements — are powerful evidence: *assertion does work!* And there may be no more important arena for its application than overcoming the sense of "What's the use? I can't make a difference," that tends to pervade the realm of personal political action.

Sadly, of course, social institutions change slowly. Colleges and universities, governments, political institutions, and international conglomerate corporations often resist change until conditions become so oppressive that some people consider it necessary to become aggressive in pursuit of their goals. They may take to the streets in violent protest, vandalize property, or even hurt other people in order to make a point.

Yet such institutions tend to dig in and resist violent change; they are most likely to respond favorably to persistent *assertive* action.

Since we've been carefully taught by family, school, and society not to speak up or demand even reasonable rights, we may feel powerless to express ourselves, or highly anxious if we do stand up to be counted. It's time for families, schools, businesses, churches, and governments to encourage individual self-assertion, and to stop limiting self-fulfilling actions. It is our hope that frustrated individuals and groups seeking change will elect to employ assertive alternatives in pursuit of their goals.

After all, *each of us has the right to be and to express ourselves, and to feel good (not powerless or guilty) about doing so, as long as we do not hurt others in the process.*

How Are You Assertive Now?

There is no greatness where there is not
simplicity, goodness, and truth.
— LEO TOLSTOI

W HAT DO YOU KNOW about your own assertiveness? Others' reactions give you clues: Aunt Maria says, "You're sassy!" The boss tells you to be more forceful with customers. Or perhaps the children believe you need to "tell off" the mechanic. Maybe you tried to speak up to a clerk, who responded with a scornful look.

While everyday comments and reactions such as these are helpful indications of your progress in assertiveness, we hope you'll be more thorough and systematic in observing yourself.

We should first point out to you that assertiveness is one of the toughest problems trainers and trainees have faced since assertiveness training got started. Many, many tests have been developed. None really does the job thoroughly and accurately.

The *Assertiveness Inventory* on the following two pages is not perfect either, but we think you'll find it a helpful tool as you improve your understanding and awareness of yourself.

ASSERTIVENESS INVENTORY
Robert E. Alberti, Ph.D. and Michael L. Emmons, Ph.D.

The following questions will be helpful in assessing your assertiveness. Be honest in your responses. All you have to do is draw a circle around the number that describes you best. For some questions the assertive end of the scale is at 0, for others at 3. Key: 0 means **no** or **never**; 1 means **somewhat** or **sometimes**; 2 means **usually** or **a good deal**; and 3 means **practically always** or **entirely**.

1. When a person is highly unfair, do you call it to attention?	0 1 2 3
2. Do you find it difficult to make decisions?	0 1 2 3
3. Are you openly critical of others' ideas, opinions, behavior?	0 1 2 3
4. Do you speak out in protest when someone takes your place in line?	0 1 2 3
5. Do you often avoid people or situations for fear of embarrassment?	0 1 2 3
6. Do you usually have confidence in your own judgement?	0 1 2 3
7. Do you insist that your spouse or roommate take on a fair share of household chores?	0 1 2 3
8. Are you prone to "fly off the handle?"	0 1 2 3
9. When a salesperson makes an effort, do you find it hard to say "No" even though the merchandise is not really what you want?	0 1 2 3
10. When a latecomer is waited on before you are, do you call attention to the situation?	0 1 2 3
11. Are you reluctant to speak up in a discussion or debate?	0 1 2 3
12. If a person has borrowed money (or a book, garment, thing of value) and is overdue in returning it, do you mention it?	0 1 2 3
13. Do you continue to pursue an argument after the other person has had enough?	0 1 2 3
14. Do you generally express what you feel?	0 1 2 3
15. Are you disturbed if someone watches you at work?	0 1 2 3

16. If someone keeps kicking or bumping your chair in a movie
    or a lecture, do you ask the person to stop?   0 1 2 3

17. Do you find it difficult to keep eye contact when talking
    to another person?   0 1 2 3

18. In a good restaurant, when your meal is improperly prepared
    or served, do you ask the waiter/waitress to correct the situation?   0 1 2 3

19. When you discover merchandise is faulty, do you return it
    for an adjustment?   0 1 2 3

20. Do you show your anger by name-calling or obscenities?   0 1 2 3

21. Do you try to be a wallflower or a piece of the furniture in
    social situations?   0 1 2 3

22. Do you insist that your property manager (mechanic,
    repairman, etc.) make repairs, adjustments or replacements
    which are his/her responsibility?   0 1 2 3

23. Do you often step in and make decisions for others?   0 1 2 3

24. Are you able to express love and affection openly?   0 1 2 3

25. Are you able to ask your friends for small favors or help?   0 1 2 3

26. Do you think you always have the right answer?   0 1 2 3

27. When you differ with a person you respect, are you able
    to speak up for your own viewpoint?   0 1 2 3

28. Are you able to refuse unreasonable requests made by friends?   0 1 2 3

29. Do you have difficulty complimenting or praising others?   0 1 2 3

30. If you are disturbed by someone smoking near you, can you say so?   0 1 2 3

31. Do you shout or use bullying tactics to get others to do as you wish?   0 1 2 3

32. Do you finish other people's sentences for them?   0 1 2 3

33. Do you get into physical fights with others, especially with strangers?   0 1 2 3

34. At family meals, do you control the conversation?   0 1 2 3

35. When you meet a stranger, are you the first to introduce yourself
    and begin a conversation?   0 1 2 3

The real problem in measuring assertiveness, of course, is that it is such an elusive concept. There is no one single human characteristic you can put a finger on and say, "*That's assertiveness!*" It is a complex phenomenon, which depends on both the persons involved and the particular situation.

A thorough assessment of assertiveness would be based on a better definition of the concept than we currently have. And it would take into account the four dimensions we have discussed: situations, attitudes, behaviors, and obstacles. A simple paper-and-pencil test can hardly do it justice!

That doesn't mean that we ought to quit trying to figure out how we're doing in assertive self-expression. It can be very valuable to take a close look at your life and identify your strengths and weaknesses. Just don't try to lump those all together and say, "I scored 73. I must be pretty assertive!"

Take a few minutes right now to respond to the *Assertiveness Inventory*. This is just for you, so be honest with yourself. After you complete the *Inventory*, read on for the discussion of results, and for specific steps you can take to make the results practical in your life. The *Inventory* is not a "psychological test," so just relax and enjoy this brief exploration of when and how you express yourself.

You'll find the *Inventory* less than perfect, of course. Some items won't apply to your life. And you may want to respond, "*What does that mean?*" or, "*It depends on the situation.*" Don't let your criticism of the questions get in the way. If you'll take the time to answer the honestly, the *Inventory* can be a helpful tool in your growth in assertiveness.

"WHADJAGET?"

When you complete the *Inventory*, you'll probably be tempted to add up your total score. *Don't!* A "total score" really has no meaning, since no general quality of "assertiveness" has been identified by research. As you will recall from earlier chapters, and as you have no doubt experienced in your own life, "what is assertive" must be answered in terms of the person and the situation.

As we noted above, the *Inventory* is not a standardized psychological test; the studies required to thoroughly evaluate and approve a test have not been conducted. Thus, a "total score" approach is not appropriate.

Analyzing Your Results

We suggest the following steps for analysis of your responses to the Assertiveness Inventory:

❖ Look at individual events in your life, involving particular people or groups, and consider your strengths and shortcomings accordingly.

❖ Look at your responses to questions 1, 2, 4, 5, 6, 7, 9, 10, 11, 12, 14, 15, 16, 17, 18, 19, 21, 22, 24, 25, 27, 28, 30, and 35. These questions are oriented toward nonassertive behavior. Do your answers to these items tell you that you are rarely speaking up for yourself? Or are there perhaps some specific situations which give you trouble?

❖ Look at your responses to questions 3, 8, 13, 20, 23, 26, 29, 31, 32, 33, and 34. These questions are oriented toward aggressive behavior. Do your answers to these questions suggest you are pushing others around more than you realized?

Most people confirm from completing these three steps that assertiveness is situational in their lives. No one is nonassertive *all* the time, aggressive all the time, assertive all the time! Each person behaves in each of the three ways at various times, depending upon the situation. It is possible that you have a *characteristic style* that leans heavily in one direction. You may discover your own weak spot, and thereby begin the process of change.

❖ Re-read the *Inventory* and write in your log a discussion of your feelings about each item. An example:

Question 1. When a person is highly unfair, do you call it to attention?

Response: O

Discussion: I'm afraid that if I said anything, the other person would become very angry. Perhaps I'd lose a friend, or maybe the person would yell at me. That would upset me a lot.

❖ Go over all of the information you have generated from the preceding steps, and begin drawing some general conclusions. Look specifically at four aspects of the information:

... What *situations* give you trouble? Which can you handle easily?

... What are your *attitudes* about expressing yourself? Does it generally feel "right" to you?

... What *obstacles* are in the way of your assertions? Are you afraid of the consequences? Do other people in your life make it especially difficult to be assertive?

... Are your *behavior skills* up to the job? Can you be expressive when you need to be?

Examine these four areas carefully. Write comments in your log, summarizing your observations of yourself. If you'll spend some time now, thinking about these aspects of your own style of self-expression, it will help you to see your own needs more clearly, to set goals for yourself, and to determine where to go from here in your assertiveness training program.

Keep Track of Your Growth

*Where I was born and where and how I have
lived is unimportant. It is what I have done with
where I have been that should be of interest.*
— GEORGIA O'KEEFFE

W E'D LIKE TO ENCOURAGE YOU to get started now on your own process of growth toward more effective self-expression by starting a "personal growth log." Nothing fancy, just a simple device for jotting notes about how things are going in your life as you take this journey toward greater assertiveness.

As a nautical device, a log is used as a daily record of a ship's progress toward its destination. A daily record of your assertiveness will help you judge your progress over time. After a few weeks, you'll find it provides a wealth of information about your ongoing assertiveness.

We urge you to get a special notebook, pad, folder, whatever, so you can record your thoughts, observations, feelings, and progress.

Your log entries can include self-examination, notes on your reading, goals, . . . anything you'd like to keep track of. Give at least some space to five dimensions of your life which relate to assertiveness: *situations* that come up; *people* in your life; your own *attitudes*, *thoughts*, and *beliefs*; your *behaviors*; and *obstacles* to expressing yourself.

A sample page of your log might look like this:

PERSONAL GROWTH LOG FOR _____ (date)

Situations
_____
_____
_____

People
_____
_____

Attitudes/Thoughts/Beliefs
_____
_____
_____

Behaviors
_____
_____
_____

Obstacles
_____
_____

Notes (Progress/Problems/Comments/Goals)
_____
_____
_____

If you'll keep it up regularly, your log can become a very important tool for your growth program — both to record your progress and to serve as a "motivator" to continue working on your personal development.

As you undertake specific changes in your life, you may wish to become more thorough in your log-keeping. The ideas which follow may be of some help.

❖ You may wish to refer to the *Assertiveness Inventory* (chapter 3). Which *situations* and *people* can you handle effectively and which are troublesome? Write down the results in your log. Pay particular attention to any patterns in your life. Are you more assertive with strangers than with intimates, for example, or perhaps vice versa? Can you readily stand up for your rights, but fall down on expressing affection? Do such factors as age, sex, or roles (e.g., authority) of the other person make a difference?

❖ It is very difficult to accurately measure *attitudes*, and particularly difficult to be objective about your own. Nevertheless, we encourage you to write down in your log your feelings about your right to behave assertively. Look at the various situations and people in the definition of assertive behavior (chapter 2), and in the situations described in the *Assertiveness Inventory* (chapter 3). For example, do you feel that it's okay to respond when you've been criticized by a boss or teacher?

❖ Evaluating your *behavior* is not as difficult, but may take longer. In chapter 6, we'll describe in detail several components of behavior which are part of any assertive act. If you watch your own behavior carefully for a time (a week or more is a good idea), and record your observations regularly in your log, you will have a good idea of your own effectiveness with eye contact, facial expression, body posture, and the other components. It may help to watch some other people you consider effectively assertive, and to note in your log some of their behavioral qualities as well.

❖ *Obstacles* may be the easiest area for you to keep track of. Most people want to act assertively, but there are many barriers which seem to make assertion difficult. Common obstacles within you fall into two categories: anxiety — fear of the possible consequences (Maybe the other person won't like me, or will hit me, or will think I'm crazy; or maybe I'll make a fool of myself; or maybe I'll fail to get what I want; or maybe I just feel anxious!); and lack of skills (I don't know how to meet girls. What do I do to express a political opinion? I never learned how to show affection.).

Perhaps the most difficult external obstacles are the other people in your life. (Parents, friends, lovers, roommates, and others have an interest in making it difficult for you to change, even if they believe they want you to be more assertive).

Record in your log those obstacles which you think are making assertiveness more difficult for you.

MAKING YOUR LOG WORK FOR YOU

If you will take the time and effort to keep a log and, as you learn more about assertiveness, to proceed carefully and thoroughly with your self-assessment, you will find that the results will help to pinpoint specifically what you will need to do to increase your assertiveness. At every point, of course, you may choose whether to carry this personal growth program further, and what direction you will take. And choice is the key element in your assertiveness anyway!

Every week or so, carefully examine your log entries: situations, attitudes, behaviors, obstacles, notes. Look for patterns. Remember to evaluate your strengths as well as your weaknesses.

The first week or two of entries in your log should give you a good picture of how you are doing now, and provide a basis for setting goals for yourself. While we have not yet presented a systematic process for setting goals (that comes in chapter 8), we encourage you to continue to think about your own hopes for improved assertiveness, and to make notes in your log about them.

Your log might show you that you have difficulty with people in authority — that you don't believe you have a right to speak up to them, that you can't maintain good eye contact with them, and that you're very anxious around such people. You can work on these items individually through the step-by-step procedures described in this book.

Changing long-standing behaviors, aggressive, nonassertive, or others, is difficult. Your log can be a crucial asset in the process of change. As you become aware of your behavior patterns, you can begin to choose deliberately, and act in ways that will move you toward your goals. As your initial awkward attempts at assertion are rewarded — "Hey, it worked!" — you'll find the assertive choice will become easier and easier.

Start your log today with notes about your reading thus far in the book. Keep using your log throughout your reading of *Your Perfect Right* and beyond, to keep a careful record of how you're doing as you apply these concepts in your own life. Your log will provide a series of "bench marks" so you can watch yourself grow. It will help motivate you to work at your progress. It will remind you how far you really have come — especially valuable at those times when you begin to think you aren't getting anywhere! Reading your log will reassure you that you are making progress, even if it is slow.

Your log will help you to be more systematic about your work on assertiveness. And that can make all the difference!

As you learn new things about yourself, you may find complex and severe shortcomings in some of the behavioral areas we've discussed. In that case, you may want some professional assistance in reaching your goal. Particularly if you experience very high levels of anxiety about being assertive, we suggest contact with a qualified counselor, psychologist, psychiatrist, or other therapist. Your local community mental health center or college/university counseling center can assist you in finding someone to help.

Part II

Discovering
Assertiveness

What It Means
to Be Assertive

There are three possible broad approaches
to the conduct of interpersonal relations.
The first is to consider one's self only
and ride roughshod over others . . .
The second . . . is always to put others
before one's self . . .The third approach is
the golden mean . . .The individual
places himself first, but
takes others into account.
— JOSEPH WOLPE

STOP TEN PEOPLE ON THE STREET and ask them what it means to be assertive. You'll get ten answers, with little agreement.

"What's this? We're only to chapter 5 and you're already telling us you don't know what you're talking about?"

Not exactly. What we are saying is that assertiveness often seems simple on the surface, but looked at in detail — "under a microscope" — it suddenly becomes complex. While you don't need to understand all its intricacies in order to use it, it's like an automobile or computer: it does help to have an idea what goes on "under the hood."

So in this chapter, we'll take a look the concept of assertiveness, beginning with our brief definition from chapter 2:

Assertive behavior promotes equality in human relationships, enabling us to act in our own best interests, to stand up for ourselves without undue anxiety, to express feelings honestly and comfortably, to exercise personal rights without denying the rights of others.

Let's examine those elements in greater detail:

To promote equality in human relationships means to put both parties on an equal footing, to restore the balance of power by giving personal power to the "underdog," to make it possible for everyone to gain and no one to lose.

To act in your own best interests refers to the ability to make your own decisions about career, relationships, life style and time schedule, to take initiative starting conversations and organizing activities, to trust your own judgment, to set goals and work to achieve them, to ask help from others, to participate socially.

To stand up for yourself includes such behaviors as saying no, setting limits on time and energy, responding to criticism or put-downs or anger, expressing or supporting or defending an opinion.

To express feelings honestly and comfortably means the ability to disagree, to show anger, to show affection or friendship, to admit fear or anxiety, to express agreement or support, to be spontaneous — all without painful anxiety.

To exercise personal rights relates to competency as a citizen, as a consumer, as a member of an organization or school or work group, as a participant in public events to express opinions, to work for change, to respond to violations of one's own rights or those of others.

To not deny the rights of others is to accomplish the above personal expressions without unfair criticism of others, without hurtful behavior toward others, without name-calling, without intimidation, without manipulation, without controlling others.

Putting those elements of the definition back together, you can see that assertive behavior is a positive self-affirmation which also values the other people in your life. It contributes both to your personal life satisfaction and to the quality of your relationships with others.

Studies show that, as a direct result of gains in self-expressiveness, individuals have improved their self-esteem, reduced their anxiety, overcome depression, gained greater respect from others, accomplished more in terms of their life goals, increased their level of self-understanding, and improved their capacity to communicate more effectively with others. We can't promise any specific results for you, of course, but the evidence is impressive!

ASSERTIVE, NONASSERTIVE, AND AGGRESSIVE BEHAVIOR

Life in the twenty-first century presents mixed messages about appropriate behavior. Typical examples of conflicts between *recommended* and *rewarded* behavior are evident in many areas of life. Even though it is generally stated that one should respect the rights of others, all too often we observe that parents, teachers, business and government contradict these values in their own actions. Tact, diplomacy, politeness, refined manners, modesty, and self-denial are generally praised; yet to get ahead it is often acceptable to step on others.

The athlete who participates in competitive sports is encouraged to be aggressive, perhaps even to bend the rules a little. That's OK, because "It's not important how you play the game; it's just important that you win." Contrast the rewards for winning coaches with those for losing coaches who "build character." Woody Hayes, much-acclaimed former head football coach at Ohio State University, is quoted as saying, "Show me a good loser, and I'll show you a loser."

So, how to deal with these mixed messages? We believe you should be able to *choose for yourself* how to act. If your "polite restraint" response is too strong, you may be unable to express yourself as you would like. If your aggressive response is overdeveloped, you may achieve your goals by hurting others. Freedom of choice and self-control are possible when you develop assertive responses for situations you have previously handled nonassertively or aggressively.

> *Assertive behavior is a positive self-affirmation which also values the other people in your life.*

Let's contrast assertive, nonassertive and aggressive actions to help clarify these concepts. The chart on the next page displays several feelings and consequences typical for the person (*sender*) whose actions are nonassertive, assertive, or aggressive. Also shown, for each of these actions, are the likely consequences for the person toward whom the action is directed (*receiver*).

As the chart on the next page shows, a nonassertive response means that the sender is denying self-expression, and is inhibited from letting feelings show. People who behave nonassertively often feel hurt and anxious since they allow others to choose for them. They seldom achieve their own desired goals.

The person who carries a desire for self-expression to the extreme of *aggressive* behavior accomplishes goals at the expense of others. Although frequently self-enhancing and expressive of feelings in the situation, aggressive behavior hurts other people in the process by making choices for them and by minimizing their worth.

Aggressive behavior commonly results in a *putdown* of the receiver. Rights denied, the receiver feels hurt, defensive, and humiliated. His or her goals in the situation, of course, are not achieved. Aggressive behavior may achieve the sender's goals, but may also generate bitterness and frustration which may later return as vengeance.

NON-ASSERTIVE BEHAVIOR	AGGRESSIVE BEHAVIOR	ASSERTIVE BEHAVIOR
Sender	**Sender**	**Sender**
Self-denying	Self-enhancing at expense of another	Self-enhancing
Inhibited		Expressive
Hurt, anxious	Expressive	Feels good about self
Allows others to choose	Chooses for others	Chooses for self
Does not achieve desired goal	Achieves desired goal by hurting others	May achieve desired goal
Receiver	**Receiver**	**Receiver**
Guilty or angry	Self-denying	Self-enhancing
Depreciates sender	Hurt, defensive, humiliated	Expressive
Achieves desired goal at sender's expense	Does not achieve desired goal	May achieve desired goal

Some professionals who work with assertiveness training prefer to add a fourth category — *indirect aggression* — to this model. They note that much aggressive behavior takes the form of passive, non-confrontive action. Sometimes such actions are sneaky or sly, other times they may simply be *double entendre*. Characteristic of this style is the smiling, friendly, agreeable behavior which hides a back-stabbing or undermining action. We consider this category to be a form of aggression, and have simplified our model by not dealing with it separately. We do acknowledge its importance, however, and will have more to say about it in chapter 18.

Appropriately *assertive* behavior in the same situation would be self-enhancing for the sender, an honest expression of feelings, and will usually achieve the goal. When you choose for yourself how to act, a good feeling typically accompanies the assertive response, even when your goals are not achieved.

Similarly, when the consequences of these three contrasting behaviors are viewed from the perspective of the receiver the action, we see a parallel pattern in the chart. Nonassertive behavior often produces feelings ranging from sympathy to confusion to outright contempt for the sender. Also, the receiver may feel guilt or anger at having achieved goals at the sender's expense. The receiver of aggressive actions often feels hurt, defensive, put-down, or perhaps aggressive in return. In contrast, assertion tends to enhance the feeling of self-worth of both parties, and permits both full self-expression and achievement of goals.

In summary, it is clear that the sender is hurt by self-denial in nonassertive behavior; the receiver (or even both parties) may be hurt by aggressive behavior. In the case of assertion, neither person is hurt, and it is likely that both will succeed. The series of example situations which appears in the following chapter will help to make these distinctions more clear.

It is important to note that assertive behavior is *person-and-situation-specific*, not universal. That is, what may be considered assertive depends upon the persons involved and the circumstances of the situation. Although we believe the definitions and examples presented in this book are realistic and appropriate for most people and circumstances, individual differences must be considered. Cultural or ethnic background for example, may create an entirely different set of personal circumstances which would change the nature of "appropriateness" in assertive behavior.

CULTURAL DIFFERENCES IN SELF-ASSERTION

While the desire for self-expression may be a basic human need, assertive behavior in interpersonal relationships is primarily characteristic of western cultures. (For purposes of illustration, please permit us a few cultural generalizations and a stereotype or two.)

In many Asian cultures, group membership (family, clan, workgroup) and "face" are highly valued. How one is seen by others tends to be more important to an individual than is self-concept. Politeness is a key virtue, and communication is often indirect so as to avoid confrontation or offending one another. Assertiveness, in the Western sense of direct self-expression, is generally not considered appropriate by those who value tradition. Many young people, however, and those whose business activities include considerable contact with the U.S. and Europe, have developed more direct, informal, and assertive styles.

Many individuals and subcommunities in Latin and Hispanic societies have emphasized the notion of "machismo" to the point that assertiveness — as we have defined it — seems rather tame, especially for men. In those cases, a greater display of strength is the norm for male self-expression.

Yet, people from cultures where self-assertion traditionally has not been valued may be just those who most need its benefits. As our world shrinks, it may be that current and future international relations require more open and direct communication, and a greater sense of equality — expressed on both sides of the table.

"But Isn't Aggression Just Human Nature?"

Aggression and violence are often excused on the grounds that they are innate in the human organism, and cannot be avoided. Not so, say the most distinguished scholars who have researched the subject. The "Seville Statement" — written in 1986 by 20 distinguished social and behavioral scientists from 12 nations, and endorsed by the American Psychological and American Anthropological Associations — says:

"It is *scientifically incorrect* to say . . .

❖ ". . . we have inherited a tendency to make war from our animal ancestors. Warfare is a peculiarly human phenomenon and does not occur in other animals. War is biologically possible, but it is not inevitable . . .

❖ ". . . that war or any other violent behavior is genetically programmed into our human nature. Except for rare pathologies the genes do not produce individuals necessarily predisposed to violence. Neither do they determine the opposite.

❖ ". . . that humans have a 'violent brain.' While we do have the neural apparatus to act violently, there is nothing in our neurophysiology that compels (such behavior).

❖ ". . . that war is caused by 'instinct' or any single motivation . . .

"We conclude that biology does not condemn humanity to war, and that humanity can be freed from the bondage of biological pessimism. Violence is neither in our evolutionary legacy nor in our genes. The same species (that) invented war is capable of inventing peace."

Classifying Behavior: "A Rose, By Any Other Name . . ."

"I told my father-in-law not to smoke his cigar in my house. Was that assertive or aggressive?"

Members of assertiveness training groups and workshops often ask trainers to classify a particular act as "assertive" or "aggressive." What criteria do make the important difference?

We have suggested that assertive and aggressive behavior differ principally in that the latter involves hurting, manipulating, or denying others in the course of expressing oneself.

Practitioners and writers with a psychoanalytic orientation have proposed that *intent* must be considered. That is, if you intended to hurt your father-in-law, that's aggressive; if you simply wanted to inform him of your wishes, you were acting assertively.

Many psychologists insist that behavior must be measurable according to its *effects*. Thus, if your father gets the assertive message and responds accordingly — by agreeing not to smoke — your behavior may be classified as assertive. If he pouts in a corner, or shouts, "Who do you think you are?" your statement may have been aggressive, as described by this criterion.

Finally, as we have noted, the *social-cultural context* must be taken into account in classifying behavior as assertive or aggressive or nonassertive. A culture, for example, which regards honoring one's elders as one of its ultimate values may view the request as clearly out of line and aggressive, regardless of the behavior, response, or intent.

There are no absolutes in this area, and some criteria may be in conflict. A particular act may be at once assertive in *behavior* and *intent* (you wanted to and did express your feelings), aggressive in response (the other person could not handle your assertion), and nonassertive in the social context (your culture expects a powerful, put-down style). It's not always easy to classify human behavior!

A specific situation may vary considerably from the examples we discuss here. In any event, the question "Is it assertive or aggressive?" is not one which may be answered simply! Each situation ultimately must be evaluated on its own. The labels "nonassertive," "assertive," and "aggressive" themselves carry no magic, but they may be useful in assessing the appropriateness of a particular action.

Our concern is not with the labels, but with helping you to *choose for yourself* how you will act, and with helping you know that you have the tools you need to succeed.

SOCIAL CONSEQUENCES OF ASSERTION

While it is our purpose in *Your Perfect Right* to teach you skills so that you may improve your own ability to express yourself appropriately and responsibly, we believe strongly that self-expression must be modulated by its context. Just as freedom of speech does not convey the right to yell "fire" in a crowded theater, so the form of self-expression we advocate is one which considers its consequences.

The perfect right you have to say "no" exists alongside the other person's right to say "yes." And your desire to accomplish your goals through self-assertion must be weighed against the needs of the larger society. Speak out or write about any idea you choose to support, but recognize the other person's right to do the same. And be prepared to pay some dues — perhaps in jail — if your expression goes beyond words and includes civil disobedience. Just as there are taxes for those who accumulate wealth, there is a price to pay for freedom of expression.

While you have a perfect right to advocate a viewpoint, everyone else has the same right — and your views may conflict. Keep this in mind on your journey toward greater personal assertiveness.

ASSERTIVENESS IN A NEW MILLENNIUM

In early editions of *Your Perfect Right*, we used the following example of a situation calling for assertive action: *"Has anyone ever cut in front of you in a line?"* Our advice, of course, was to speak up for yourself, to call attention to the situation, to ask that the line-jumper respect the rights of those who have already been waiting. Today, frankly, we're not so sure.

For over 30 years, through seven editions and over a million copies of this book, we have emphasized the importance of individual self-expression, and our commitment to the value of each individual human being has not wavered. But we would like to comment on a few of the realities in which we find ourselves in the U.S.A. today.

We have long considered appropriate assertiveness to be "person and situation-specific." The cutting-in-line situation must be assessed more carefully today than 25 years ago. Our "perfect rights" haven't changed, of course, but our right to express them must be exercised with greater caution. It has always been true that you risk being punched in the nose when you speak up for yourself. Today, however, the probability of a violent reaction seems greater than ever before. A punch in the nose, an obscene gesture, even a knife or gun are seen as the quick answer to many disagreements.

Cut me off on the freeway? The least you'll get is my horn and the extended digit of my free hand. You may get bumped the next time traffic slows down. Or I may just decide to run you off the road.

Reprimand or fire me at work? I may return with a gun to "pay you back," if I'm emotionally unstable or wigged out on drugs. (Law enforcement officials tell us that a huge percentage of convicted criminals are chronic drug users.)

There are, of course, no easy answers to such dilemmas of life in a violence-prone society. We cannot recommend that you take the risks of asserting yourself under all circumstances, nor will we advise you to duck inside your shell and avoid any situation in which your safety may be at stake. What we do advocate is that you exercise appropriate caution in risky situations. Take time to consider the possible consequences of your actions, how well you know the person(s) you're dealing with, how well you know the territory in which you find yourself, how important it is to have your say, whether you're likely to accomplish anything by speaking up, etc.

In chapter 19, we've elaborated on those thoughts, and put together a checklist of criteria to aid you in making the decision, "Is this a situation in which I want to be assertive?"

Don't misunderstand our caveat here. We do not want you to avoid reasonable assertions because there may be risk. There is risk in getting out of bed in the morning. There is risk in driving your car (even without the "crazies"). There is risk in most jobs (ask your employer about the cost of Worker's Compensation insurance, even for "non-hazardous" jobs!). There is risk in living in the city — or in the country. There is risk in involving yourself in a relationship.

To avoid risk is to avoid life — and we want you to live as fully as you can. As psychologist and philosopher William James said, "Live all you can; it's a mistake not to." Just consider taking risks that count for something!

Our society needs all the help it can get in creating harmony. Let's focus our assertiveness where it's meaningful, working toward equality and cooperation in relationships with others.

Ten Key Points About Assertive Behavior

To summarize this chapter, here is a list of ten key qualities of assertive behavior.

Assertive behavior is:

1. *Self-expressive*;
2. *Respectful* of the rights of others;
3. *Honest*;
4. *Direct and firm*;
5. *Equalizing*, benefitting both parties in a relationship;
6. Both *verbal* (including the content of the message), and *nonverbal* (including the style of the message);
7. *Positive* at times (expressing affection, praise, appreciation), and negative at times (expressing limits, anger, criticism);
8. *Appropriate for the person and situation*, not universal;
9. *Socially responsible*;
10. *Learned*, not inborn.

Now you have a better idea of what it means to be assertive, and you are probably ready to begin taking steps toward increasing your own assertiveness.

The following chapter provides many examples of life situations calling for assertive action. It's likely you'll find yourself nodding in recognition as you read some of these!

6

"Can You Give Me an Example?"

*We are all controlled by the world
in which we live. . . . The question is this:
are we to be controlled by accidents,
by tyrants, or by ourselves?*
— B.F. SKINNER

LOOK AT SOME EVERYDAY SITUATIONS will improve your understanding of the behavioral styles we've discussed. As you read the examples in this chapter, you may wish to pause and think about your own response before reading the alternative responses we have presented. These examples are oversimplified, of course, so we can demonstrate the ideas more clearly.

DINING OUT

Akim and Letitia are at dinner in a moderately expensive restaurant. Akim has ordered grilled chicken breast; but when the steak is served, he finds it overcooked and dry. His action is:

Nonassertive: Akim grumbles to Letitia about the "burned" meat, and vows that he won't patronize this restaurant in the future. He says nothing to the waitress, responding "Fine!" to her inquiry, "Is everything all right?" His dinner and evening are spoiled, and he feels angry with himself for taking no action. Akim's estimate of himself and Letitia's estimate of him are both deflated by the experience.

Aggressive: Akim angrily summons the waitress to his table. He berates her loudly and unfairly for not complying with his order. His actions ridicule the waitress and embarrass Letitia. He demands and receives another chicken breast, this one more to his liking. He feels in control of the situation, but Letitia's embarrassment creates friction between them and spoils their night out. The waitress is humiliated and angry for the rest of the evening.

Assertive: Akim motions the waitress to his table. He shows her the overcooked meat, and asks politely but firmly that it be returned to the kitchen and replaced. The waitress apologizes for the error, and shortly returns with a properly cooked order of chicken. Akim and Letitia enjoy dinner and Akim feels satisfaction with himself. The waitress is pleased with a satisfied customer and a generous tip.

Something Borrowed

Yolanda is an airline flight attendant, bright, outgoing, and a good worker liked by customers and peers. She lives in a condo with two roommates, and is looking forward to a quiet evening at home one Friday when her roommate Mary asks a favor. Mary says that she is going out with a special man, and wants to borrow Yolanda's new and quite expensive necklace. The necklace was a gift from her brother, with whom Yolanda is very close, and it means a great deal to her. Her response is:

Nonassertive: She swallows her anxiety about loss or damage to the necklace. Although she feels that its special meaning makes it too personal to lend, she says "Sure!" She denies herself, rewards Mary for making an unreasonable request, and worries all evening.

Aggressive: Yolanda is outraged at her friend's request, tells her "Absolutely not!" and rebukes her severely for even daring to ask "such a stupid question." She humiliates Mary and makes a fool of herself too. Later she feels uncomfortable and guilty. Mary's hurt feelings show all evening, and she has a miserable time, which puzzles and dismays her date. Thereafter, the relationship between Yolanda and Mary becomes very strained.

Assertive: Yolanda explains the significance of the necklace to her roommate. Politely but firmly, she observes that the request is an unreasonable one since this piece of jewelry is particularly personal. Mary is disappointed but understanding, and Yolanda feels good for having been honest. Mary impresses her date just by being herself.

Have a Snort!

Caitlin is a friendly, socially active graduate student who has been going out with Paulo, and has come to care a lot for him. One evening, he invites her to attend a small get-together with two other couples. As everyone gets acquainted at the party, Caitlin is enjoying herself. After an hour or so, one of the new friends brings out a small bag of cocaine. Everyone responds eagerly except Caitlin. She has not tried coke, and does not wish to experiment. She is in real conflict because Paulo offers her a snort. She decides to be:

Nonassertive: She accepts the cocaine and pretends to have used it before. She carefully watches the others to see how they inhale the drug. She dreads the possibility they may ask her to take more. Caitlin is worried about what her friend is thinking about her. She has denied her feelings, been dishonest with Paulo, and feels remorseful for giving in to something she did not wish to do.

Aggressive: Caitlin is visibly upset when offered the cocaine and blasts Paulo for bringing her to a party of this type. She demands he take her home right away. When the others at the party say that she does not have to use if she doesn't wish to, she yells at them. As she continues to behave indignantly, Paulo is humiliated, embarrassed before his friends, and disappointed in her. Although he remains cordial toward Caitlin as he takes her home, he bad-mouths her to his friends the next day.

Assertive: Caitlin does not accept the cocaine, replying simply, "No, I don't want it." She asks Paulo to take her home. On the way, she makes clear to him her concern that he didn't tell her in advance that cocaine would be offered at the party. She emphasizes that he also had exposed her to possible arrest, had the party been discovered by the police. Caitlin tells Paulo she'll break off the relationship if he continues to use drugs.

THE HEAVYWEIGHT

Dominic and Gina, married nine years, have been having marital problems recently because he insists that she is overweight and needs to reduce. He brings the subject up continually, pointing out that she is no longer the woman he married (she was 25 pounds lighter then). He keeps telling her that such overweight is bad for her health, that she is a bad example for the children, and so on.

Dominic teases Gina about being "chunky," looks longingly at thin women, while commenting how attractive they look, and makes reference to her figure in front of their friends. Dominic has been acting this way for several months and Gina is highly upset. She has been attempting to lose weight for months, with little success. Following Dominic's most recent rash of criticism, Gina is:

Nonassertive: She apologizes for her overweight, makes feeble excuses, or simply doesn't reply to some of Dominic's comments. Internally, she feels both hostile toward her husband for his nagging, and guilty about being overweight. Her feelings of anxiety make it even more difficult for her to lose weight and the battle continues.

Aggressive: Gina goes into a long tirade about how her husband isn't any great bargain anymore, either. She brings up the fact that at night he falls asleep on the couch half the time, is a lousy sex partner, and doesn't pay enough attention to her. She complains that he humiliates her in front of the children and their close friends, and that he acts like a "lecherous old man" by the way he eyes other women. In her anger, she succeeds only in wounding Dominic and driving a wedge between them by her counterattack.

Assertive: Approaching her husband when they are alone and will not be interrupted, Gina says that she feels that Dominic is right about her need to lose weight, but she does not like the way he keeps after her about the problem. She points out that she is doing her best and is having a difficult time losing the weight and maintaining the loss. He admits that his harping is ineffective, and together they work out a plan to exercise together. Dominic also resolves to reinforce her systematically for her efforts to lose weight.

THE NEIGHBOR KID

Edmond and Virginia have a two-year-old boy and a baby girl. Over the last several nights, their neighbor's son, 17, has been sitting in his car, in his own driveway, with his car stereo blaring loudly. He begins just about the time their two young children go to bed on the side of the house closest to the music. They've found it virtually impossible to get the children to sleep until the music stops. Edmond and Virginia are both disturbed and decide to be:

Nonassertive: They move the children into their own bedroom on the other side of the house, wait until the noise stops (around midnight), then transfer the children back to their own rooms. Then they go to bed much past their own usual bedtime. They quietly curse the teenager, and soon become alienated from their neighbors.

Aggressive: They call the police and protest that "one of those wild teenagers next door is creating a disturbance. " They demand that the police put a stop to the noise at once. The police do talk with the boy and his parents, who get very angry as a result of their embarrassment about the police visit. They denounce Edmond and Virginia for reporting to the police without speaking to them first, and resolve to have nothing further to do with them.

Assertive: Edmond goes over to the boy's house early one evening and tells him that his stereo is keeping the children awake at night. Edmond suggests they try to work out an arrangement which allows the boy his music, but does not disturb the children's sleep. The boy reluctantly agrees to set a lower volume during the late hours, but he appreciates Edmond's cooperative attitude. Both parties feel good about the outcome, and agree to follow up a week later to be sure it is working as agreed.

THE LOSER

Chang is a 22-year-old college dropout who works as a software developer. He lives alone in a converted loft not far from his workplace. Chang has had no dates for the past fourteen months. He left college after a series of depressing events — academic failures, a "Dear John" letter, and some painful harassment by other students in his residence hall. He has been in jail overnight for drunkenness on two recent occasions.

Yesterday, Chang received a letter from his mother inquiring about his well-being, but primarily devoted to a discussion of his brother's recent successes. Today, his supervisor criticized him harshly for a mistake which was actually the supervisor's own fault. A co-worker he admires turned down his invitation to dinner.

When he arrived at his apartment that evening, feeling particularly depressed, his landlord met him at the door with a tirade about "drunken bums" and a demand that this month's rent be paid on time. Chang's response is:

Nonassertive: He takes on himself the burden of the landlord's attack, feeling added guilt and even greater depression. A sense of helplessness overcomes him. He wonders how his brother can be so successful while he considers himself so worthless. The co-worker's rejection and the boss's criticism strengthen his opinion that he is worthless. He decides he really has nothing to live for, and begins to think about how he will commit suicide.

Aggressive: The landlord has added the final straw to Chang's burden. He becomes extremely angry and pushes the landlord out of the way in order to get into his room. Once alone, he resolves to "get" the people who have been making his life so miserable recently: the supervisor, the co-worker, the landlord, whoever. He remembers the guns he saw in the pawn shop window yesterday. . . .

Assertive: Chang responds firmly to the landlord, noting that he has paid his rent regularly, and that it is not due for another week. He reminds the landlord of a broken rail on the stairway and the plumbing repairs which were to have been accomplished weeks earlier. The following morning, after giving his life situation a great deal of thought, Chang calls the local mental health clinic to ask for help. At work, he approaches the supervisor calmly and explains the circumstances surrounding the mistake. Though somewhat defensive, the supervisor acknowledges her error and apologizes for her aggressive behavior.

RECOGNIZING YOUR OWN NONASSERTIVE AND AGGRESSIVE BEHAVIOR

The examples given in this chapter help to point out what "assertiveness" means in everyday events. Perhaps some of the situations "rang a bell" in your own life. Take a few minutes to listen honestly to yourself describe your relationships with others who are important to you. Carefully examine your contacts with parents, peers, co-workers, classmates, spouse, children, bosses, teachers, salespeople, neighbors, relatives. Who is dominant in these relationships? Are you easily taken advantage of in dealings with others? Do you usually express your feelings and ideas openly? Do you take advantage of or hurt others frequently?

Your responses to such questions provide hints which may lead you to explore in greater depth your assertive, nonassertive or aggressive behavior. If you did not complete the *Assertiveness Inventory* in chapter 3, we urge you to do so now. We think you'll find such a self-examination rewarding, and a very important step toward increasing your interpersonal effectiveness.

7

It's Not What You Say, It's How You Say It!

It takes two to speak truth —
one to speak and another to hear.
　　　　— HENRY DAVID THOREAU

SELF-EXPRESSION IS A UNIVERSAL HUMAN NEED. The form it takes is unique to each of us, of course. In this chapter, we'll take a look at the several components of behavior that go together to make up our individual styles. While individual differences "make the world go 'round," each of us can learn the skills necessary for good communication.

"I NEVER KNOW WHAT TO SAY!"

Many people view assertiveness as a verbal behavior, believing that they must have "just the right words" to handle a situation effectively. On the contrary, we've found that *how* you express an assertive message is a good deal more important than *what* you say. Although scripts of "what to say when . . ." are popular with many assertiveness trainers, that has never been our style. We're primarily concerned with encouraging honesty and directness, and much of that message is communicated *nonverbally*.

Participants in our groups and workshops have enjoyed watching us role-play a scene which makes this point clear: Bob acts as is a dissatisfied customer who wishes to return a defective copy of *Everything You Always Wanted to Know About Assertiveness, But Were Too Timid To Ask* to the bookstore; Mike is the clerk. Using essentially the same words, "I bought this book here last week, and discovered that 20 pages are missing. I'd like a good copy or my money back," Bob approaches Mike in three different ways:

1. Bob walks slowly and hesitantly to the counter. His eyes are downcast at the floor, he speaks just above a whisper, his face looks as though it belongs on the cover of the book. He has a tight grip on the book, and a "please don't hurt me" posture.

2. Bob swaggers toward the counter, glares at Mike, addresses him in a voice heard all over the store. Bob's posture and fist-like gesture are an obvious attempt to intimidate the clerk.

3. Bob walks up to the counter facing Mike. He stands relaxed and erect, smiles, and looks directly at Mike with a friendly expression. In a conversational volume and tone of voice, he states the message, gesturing to point out the flaw in the book.

The three styles are over-exaggerated in our demonstration, of course, but the point is clear. The nonassertive, self-defeating style says to Mike that this customer is a pushover, and the slightest resistance will cause him to give up and go away. The second approach may achieve the goal of refund or exchange, but the aggressive Bob will leave with Mike's hostility directed at his back! With the assertive approach, Bob gets what he came for, and Mike feels good about having helped solve a problem for an appreciative customer.

THE COMPONENTS OF ASSERTIVE BEHAVIOR

Systematic observations of assertive behavior have led behavioral scientists to conclude that there are several important components which contribute to an assertive act. Our thinking in this area was significantly influenced by the late Michael Serber, a California psychiatrist who did extensive work with assertiveness training in the 1960s and 70s.

It should be noted that most of the research in this field has been done with North Americans of European ancestry. Ethnic and cultural considerations are very important influences on the components described in this chapter. You are urged to re-read the discussion of cultural factors in chapter 2, and to be aware of cultural dimensions as you study these aspects of behavior.

With that caveat in mind, then, let's examine the key components of assertive behavior in detail:

Eye Contact. One of the most obvious aspects of behavior when talking to another person is where you look. In general, if you look directly at the person as you speak, it helps to communicate your sincerity and to increase the directness of your message. If you look down or away much of the time, you present a lack of confidence, or a quality of deference to the other person. If you stare too intently, the other person may feel an uncomfortable invasion.

We do not advocate that you *maximize* eye contact. Continuously looking at someone can make the other person uncomfortable, is inappropriate and unnecessary, and may appear to be a game. Moreover, eye contact is a cultural variable; many cultural groups limit the amount of eye contact which is acceptable, particularly between age groups or members of the opposite sex.

Nevertheless, the importance of eye contact is obvious. A relaxed and steady gaze at the other, looking away occasionally as is comfortable, helps to make conversation more personal, to show interest in and respect for the other person, and to enhance the directness of your message.

As is true with other behaviors, eye contact may be improved by conscious effort, in small steps. Be aware of your eyes as you talk with others, and attempt to gradually optimize your eye attention in conversation.

Body Posture. As you watch other people talking with each other, carefully observe how each is standing or sitting. You may be as amazed as we have been by the number of people who talk with someone while their bodies are turned away from that person.

People sitting side by side often turn only their heads toward one another while talking. Next time you are in that situation, notice how much more personal the conversation becomes with a slight turn of the torso — say 30 degrees — toward the other person.

> *There are several important components which contribute to an assertive act.*

Relative "power" in an encounter may be emphasized by standing or sitting. A particularly evident power imbalance may be seen in the relationship between a tall adult and a small child; the adult who is thoughtful enough to bend or crouch to the child's height will find an observable difference in the quality of communication, and usually a much more responsive child!

In a situation in which you are called upon to stand up for yourself, it may be useful to do just that — stand up. An active and erect posture, while facing the other person directly, lends additional assertiveness to your message. A slumped, passive stance gives the other person an immediate advantage, as does any tendency on your part to lean back or move away. Remember Bob's first approach to the "bookstore clerk" at the beginning of this chapter?

Distance/Physical Contact. An interesting aspect of cross-cultural research into nonverbal communication is that of distance vs. closeness between people in conversation. As a very broad generalization, it has been said that, among European peoples, the farther North one goes, the farther apart individuals stand when engaged in conversation. In the United States, as in Europe, closeness seems to increase in warmer climates; but there are important exceptions, notably among ethnic subcultures which value closeness and contact differently.

Closeness is, of course, not necessarily related to temperature. Cultural and social customs are products of very complex historical factors. In the Arab world, for example, it is customary for men to greet one another with a hug and kiss, and to stand very close to each other. Interestingly, however, it would be considered

What *you say must take into consideration to whom *you are* saying it.*

very inappropriate for an Arab man to behave toward a woman in this way, yet that is quite common in the United States and Southern Europe.

Distance from another person does have a considerable effect upon communication. Standing or sitting very closely, or touching, suggests intimacy in a relationship, unless the people happen to be in a crowd or very cramped quarters. The typical discomfort of elevator passengers is a classic example of the difficulty we have in dealing with closeness! Coming too close may offend the other person, make him/her defensive, or open the door to greater intimacy. It can be worthwhile to check out verbally how the other person feels about your closeness.

Gestures. Accentuating your message with appropriate gestures can add emphasis, openness, and warmth. Bob Alberti traces his enthusiastic use of gestures in conversation to his Italian heritage. While gesturing is indeed a somewhat culturally-related behavior, a relaxed use of gestures can add depth or power to your messages. Uninhibited movement can also suggest openness, self-confidence (unless the gesturing is erratic and nervous), and spontaneity on the part of the speaker.

Facial Expression. Ever see someone trying to express anger while smiling or laughing? It just doesn't come across. Effective assertions require an expression that agrees with the message. An angry message is clearest when delivered with a straight, non-smiling countenance. A friendly communication should not be delivered with a dark frown. Let your face say the same thing your words are saying!

If you will look at yourself in the mirror, you can learn a great deal about what your face says on your behalf. First, relax all the muscles of your face as much as you can. Let go of your expression, relax the muscles around your mouth, let your jaw go loose, let your cheeks soften, along with the wrinkles of your forehead and around your eyes. Pay careful attention to the relaxed, soft feelings. Now smile, bringing your mouth up as widely as you can. Feel the tightness in your cheeks, around your eyes, all the way up to your ears. Hold that smile, look at the expression in the mirror, and concentrate on the feelings of tightness. Now relax your face completely again. Notice the difference between the relaxed feelings and those of the tight smile, and the difference between the expressions you see in the mirror.

With greater awareness of how your facial muscles feel in various expressions, and of how you look when you smile and when you are relaxed, you can begin to control your facial expression more consciously, and to make it congruent with what you are thinking, feeling, or saying. And you may develop a more natural, less "plastic" smile for those times when you really want your happiness to show!

Voice Tone, Inflection, Volume. The way we use our voices is a vital element in our communications. The same words spoken through clenched teeth in anger offer an entirely different message than when they are shouted with joy or whispered in fear.

A level, well modulated, conversational statement is convincing without being intimidating. A whispered monotone will seldom convince another person that you mean business, while a shouted epithet will bring defenses into the path of communication.

Voice is one of the easiest of the components of behavior on which to gain accurate feedback these days. Most everyone has easy access to a small cassette recorder which can be used to "try out" different styles of your voice. You may wish to experiment with a conversational tone, an angry shouted blast, a caring message, a persuasive argument. You may be surprised at how quiet your "shouts" are, or at how loud your "conversational tone" is.

Consider at least three dimensions of your voice:

❖ *tone* (is it raspy, whiny, seductively soft, angry?);

❖ *inflection* (do you emphasize certain syllables, as in a question, or speak in a monotone, or with "sing-song" effect?);

❖ *volume* (do you try to gain attention with a whisper or to overpower others with loudness, or is it very difficult for you to shout even when you want to?).

If you can control and use your voice effectively, you have acquired a powerful tool in your self-expression. Practice with a recorder, trying out different styles until you achieve a style you like. Allow time for changes to come, and use the recorder regularly to check your progress.

Fluency. Psychiatrist Mike Serber employed an exercise he called "sell me something," in which he asked the client to talk persuasively about an object, such as a watch, for thirty seconds. For many people, it is very difficult to put together a string of words lasting thirty seconds.

A smooth flow of speech is a valuable asset to get your point across in any type of conversation. It is not necessary to talk rapidly for a long period; but if your speech is interrupted with long periods of hesitation, your listeners may get bored, and will probably recognize you are very unsure of yourself. Clear and slow comments are more easily understood and more powerful than rapid speech which is erratic and filled with long pauses and stammering.

Once again, the tape recorder is a valuable tool. Use the machine to practice by talking on a familiar subject for thirty seconds. Then listen to yourself, noticing pauses of three seconds or more and space fillers such as "uhhh . . ." and "you know . . ." Repeat the same exercise, more slowly if necessary, trying to eliminate any significant pauses. Gradually increase the difficulty of the task by dealing with less familiar topics, trying to be persuasive, pretending to respond in an argument, or working with a friend to keep a genuine dialog going. The program of the Toastmasters (International Trainers in Communication) organization offers a unique opportunity for practice with feedback from a supportive audience.

Assertiveness does not depend upon being highly verbal.

Timing. In general, we advocate spontaneity of expression as a goal. Nevertheless, while hesitation may diminish the effectiveness of your assertions, it is never "too late" to be assertive! Even though the ideal moment has passed, you will usually find it worthwhile to go to the person at a later time and express your feelings. Indeed, it is so important to express one's feelings that psychologists have developed special techniques to help individuals express strong emotions toward those who may have died (e.g., parents) before the feelings could be expressed.

Spontaneous assertion will help keep your life clear, and will help you to focus accurately on the feelings you have at the time. At times, however, it is necessary to choose an occasion to discuss a strong feeling. It is not a good idea to confront someone in front of others, for example, because extra defenses are sure to be present under those conditions. If you must "let it all hang out," find a private place and time to do so!

Listening. This component is perhaps the most difficult both to describe and to change, yet it may well be the most important. Assertive listening involves an active commitment to the other person. It requires your full attention, yet calls for no overt act on your part, although eye contact and certain gestures — such as nodding — are often appropriate. Listening demonstrates your respect for the other person. It requires that you avoid expressing *yourself* for a time, perhaps even putting your own needs on hold as you listen, yet is not a nonassertive act.

Listening is not simply the physical response of hearing sounds — indeed, hearing-impaired persons may be excellent "listeners." Effective listening may involve giving feedback to the other person, so that it is clear that you understood what was said.

Assertive listening requires at least these elements:

- ❖ *tuning in* to the other person, by stopping other activities, turning off the tv, ignoring other distractions, focusing your energy in his or her direction;

- ❖ *paying attention* to the message, by making eye contact if possible, nodding to show that you hear, perhaps touching her or him; and

- ❖ actively *attempting to understand* before responding, by thinking about the underlying message — the feelings behind the words — rather than trying to interpret, or to come up with an answer.

Assertiveness includes respect for the rights and feelings of others. That means assertive *receiving* — sensitivity to others — as well as assertive *sending*.

As with other components of assertive behavior, listening is a skill that can be learned. It is hard work, takes patience, and requires other people willing to work with you. Try to hook up with a "practice partner," and take turns listening to each other and sharpening each other's listening skills. Practice accurate *paraphrasing* of each other's communications, refining your paraphrases until the partner agrees you've got it right. It will strengthen your capacity to listen.

Good listening will make all of your assertions more effective, and will contribute much to the quality of your relationships.

Thoughts. Another component of assertiveness which escapes direct observation is the thinking process. Although it has long been understood intuitively that attitudes influence behavior, only recently has psychological research been sophisticated enough to deal directly with the link. Psychologists Albert Ellis of New York City and Donald Meichenbaum of Ontario, Canada, and psychiatrists Aaron Beck of Philadelphia and David Burns of the University of Pennsylvania have been particularly influential in focusing attention on the cognitive dimensions of behavior. Ellis has reduced the process to a simple A-B-C: (A) an event takes place; (B) a person sees and interprets it internally; (C) the person reacts in some way. Part B — the perception and thought process — often was ignored in the past. More recent developments in the field of "cognitive behavior therapy" have produced specific procedures for developing assertive thinking. Thus you can now work on your thoughts as well as your eye contact, posture, and gestures.

Thinking, of course, is probably the most complex thing we humans do. As you might imagine, procedures for changing our thoughts and attitudes are very complex also. We will discuss this area more in chapter 9, but for now, consider two aspects of your assertive thinking: your attitudes about whether it is a good idea in general for people to be assertive, and your thoughts about yourself when you are in a situation which calls for assertive action. Some people, for instance, think it is not a good idea for *anybody* to express himself or herself. And some say it's okay for *others*, but not for *me*. If either of these beliefs rings a bell with you, we want you to pay particular attention to chapter 9 and work on thinking assertively!

Content. We save this obvious dimension of assertiveness for last to emphasize that, although what you say is clearly important, it is often less important than most of us generally believe. We encourage honest and spontaneous expression. That means saying forcefully, "I'm damn mad about what you just did!" rather than, "You're an S.O.B.!" Again, many people hesitate because they don't know what to say. Others have found the practice of saying *something* about their feelings at the time to be a valuable step.

We encourage you to express yourself — and to take responsibility for your feelings; don't blame the other person for how you feel. Note the difference in the above example between "*I'm* mad" and "*You're* an S.O.B." It is not necessary to put the other person down (aggressive) in order to express your feeling (assertive).

You can imagine a wide variety of situations that show the importance of how you make yourself heard. The time you spend thinking about "just the right" words would be better spent making those assertions! The ultimate goal is expressing yourself, honestly and spontaneously, in a manner right for you.

Psychologists Myles Cooley and James Hollandsworth put together a model for assertive statements, made up of seven elements which are grouped into three general categories. They suggest that *saying "no" or taking a stand* includes stating your position, explaining your reason, and expressing understanding. *Asking favors or asserting rights* may be expressed by stating the problem, making a request, and getting clarification. Finally, *expressing feelings* is accomplished by a statement of your emotions in a situation. (You may find it valuable to practice each of these types of statements with your practice partner, or into a tape recorder.)

Assertiveness doesn't depend upon being highly verbal, but some folks do seem to have difficulty finding the "right words." We don't advocate particular formulas or scripts for assertive expression because we'd rather see you use your own language. The *style* of your delivery is more important than the words anyway. It's surprising how often clients tell us *very clearly* how they feel about a particular situation, and then ask, "What shall I say to the person?" Our answer is usually: "Say the same thing you just said to me!" You very likely have the "right words" without knowing it.

Dr. Suzette Haden Elgin wrote a series of books on "syntonics" — *The Gentle Art of Verbal Self-Defense* and its sequels. Elgin compares effective interpersonal communication to tuning a musical instrument. You have a standard to work toward (a tuning fork, for instance), and you must gradually adjust your tone to equal that of the standard. Likewise in communication, you can achieve your goals best by being in harmony — "syntony" — with the other person, linguistically. Your words and your non-verbal style can be fine-tuned until they match well with those of your listener.

One of the techniques of syntonics is *sensory mode-matching* — which involves recognizing and adjusting to the other person's sensory preference among seeing, hearing, touching, smelling, and tasting. Thus, one person may say, "I *see* what you mean . . ." while another means exactly the same thing when she says, "I *hear* you. . . ."

Syntonics is a creative synthesis of the work of the late family therapist Virginia Satir with the processes of Neuro-Linguistic Programming. The idea is to help us learn to "read" our audiences, and to communicate verbally and non-verbally in ways which will encourage them to respond positively to our messages. Used carefully and ethically, such procedures can be valuable tools in improved communication. (Needless to say, of course, there is plenty of room for abuse here!)

One further word about content. Psychologist Donald Cheek, a neighbor and former university faculty colleague of ours, writing about assertiveness from an African-American perspective, pointed out the need to adapt assertiveness to your cultural setting. Particularly for minorities who may find themselves in "survival" situations, he suggests that *what* you say must take into consideration *to whom* you are saying it! Language which would be interpreted as assertive within one's own subculture, for example, could easily be interpreted as aggressive by "outsiders." The issue is remarkably complex, however.

For example, cross-cultural research on facial expression suggests that different aspects of expression are both universal and culture specific. Individual differences may be greater than differences between cultural groups!

We do not advocate that you change yourself to adapt to whatever any situation seems to invite. Nevertheless, all of us do deal with individuals differently, depending upon our respective roles and the perceived "power" of others over us. We hope you can be yourself; honesty remains the best overall guide.

It is not usually the content that hangs people up. It is the anxiety, or the lack of skills, or the belief that "I have no right . . ."

We hope this chapter has caused you to think more systematically about your own self-expression, and to formulate some goals for your own work in assertiveness. To improve your familiarity with the components, and to relate each one more directly to yourself, we suggest you take a few minutes right now to assess your own strengths with a short exercise:

On a blank sheet in your log, draw eleven lines across the page, a half-inch or so apart (if your log is too small, use a couple of pages).

Label each line with one of the components described in this chapter (eye contact, facial expression, ...).

Divide each line into six segments (place a small mark in the middle, then use similar marks to divide each half into thirds).

At the top of the page, near the left end of the lines, write "I Need Work." At the top of the page, near the center of the lines, write "I'm OK." At the top of the page, near the right end of the lines, write "I'm Excellent." Here's a sample:

Now rate yourself on each component by placing marks on the lines in accordance with how well satisfied you are with your skills in each area. You may, for example, feel "OK" about your level of eye contact and the appropriateness of your facial expression in most situations, but feel your use of gestures and your voice need some work. If you really have a "way with words," you may consider your content to be "excellent." Take enough time to re-read the descriptions of the components in this chapter and to give yourself a thorough evaluation. Be sure to record this effort in your log, as we have suggested above.

Such a brief self-assessment is necessarily imprecise, and requires you to make a "global" evaluation of your skills. (Remember that assertiveness varies with situations and persons.) Nevertheless, we believe you will benefit by giving yourself this "benchmark," then referring back to it in the weeks ahead — perhaps repeating the exercise and recording it in your log from time to time — as you progress in developing greater skills in assertiveness.

The Components of Assertive Behavior

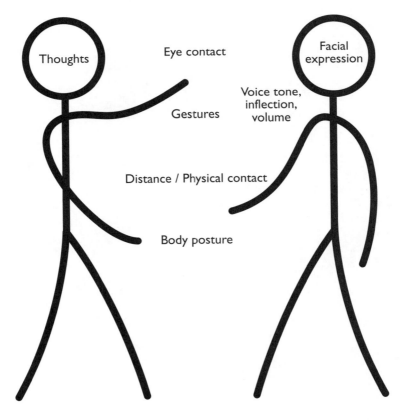

Listening ... Content ... Fluency ... Timing

Part III

Becoming Assertive

Set Goals for Yourself

Never play another person's game.
Play your own.
—ANDREW SALTER

A PROFESSOR WE ADMIRED used to tell his graduate students that changing yourself is like planning a trip: you have to find out where you are now, decide where you want to go, then figure out how to get *there* from *here*.

Much of the material in this book so far has been devoted to helping you find out where you are now in relation to assertiveness. In the following chapters we'll be focusing on ways to "get there." This chapter is the bridge — to help you decide where you're headed. Setting your goals may be the most important and most difficult step of all. Ready?

"HOW DO I KNOW WHAT I WANT?"

Assertiveness training evolved out of the idea that people live better lives if they can express what they want, if they can let others know how they would like to be treated. Some folks, however, find it hard to know what they really want from life. If you have spent most of your life doing for others, and believing that what you want is not important, it can be quite a chore to get a handle on just what is important to you!

Some people do seem to know exactly how they feel and what they want. If the neighbor's dog is barking loudly, the feeling may be annoyance or anger or fear, but such people are able to translate the feeling, get to the key issue at hand and make the needed assertions, if any.

Others find it difficult to know what their feelings are and what they want to accomplish in an encounter. They often hesitate to be assertive, lamenting "Assert *what?* I don't know what I want!" If you have such trouble you may find it valuable to try to *label* your feelings. Anger, anxiety, boredom, discomfort, and fear are common feelings. Among others you will experience are happiness, irritation, love, relaxation, sadness.

Some people will require only a few moments reflection to reveal what is being felt inside. Others may need a more active first step. It often helps to say *something* to the people involved: "I'm upset, but I'm not sure why." Or perhaps, "I'm feeling depressed." "Something feels wrong, but I can't put my finger on it." Such a statement will start you on an active search for the feeling you're sensing, and will help begin to clarify your goals.

Perhaps it is a fear of some sort which is preventing you from recognizing your feelings — a type of protective mechanism. Or you may just be so far out of touch with your feelings that you have virtually forgotten what they mean. Don't bog down at this stage. Go ahead and try to express yourself. You will probably become aware of your goal even as you proceed. Indeed, maybe all you wanted was to say something! If you do begin to recognize the underlying feeling and decide to change direction in mid-stream ("I started out angry, but realized that what I really wanted was attention!"), that is a constructive step.

You can go a long way toward clarifying your feelings in a specific situation by identifying your general life goals. Assertiveness does need direction; while it seems to be a good idea in general, it is of little value for its own sake!

You'll find at times that goals will be in conflict. You may wish, for example, to keep a friendly relationship with your next-door neighbor, but also wish to quiet his noisy dog. If you confront him about the dog, you may risk the good relationship. At such a point, clarification of your own goals will be invaluable in deciding what to do, and how to do it.

A BEHAVIORAL MODEL FOR PERSONAL GROWTH

Dr. Carl Rogers is recognized as the most influential psychological thinker of the second half of the twentieth century. His ideas were the major influence in the development of the "human potential movement." The list on the following two pages was prepared by Dr. Alberti in the early 1970s, in an attempt to translate Dr. Rogers' ideas into specific behaviors which could be carried out. We think you'll find it helpful, as you consider this matter of goals for your own growth, to read and ponder the *Behavioral Model for Personal Growth.*

STRUCTURING YOUR GOALS

OK, let's get specific. You want to write in your log (you are keeping a log, right?) a few goals which will help guide your work on assertiveness in the weeks to come. Start by thinking creatively about what you want to get out of this program of personal growth. Brainstorm about your assertiveness, writing down anything that comes to mind. Write quickly. Don't ignore or criticize any idea, no matter how silly it may seem. Be as open-minded as you can.

After you have compiled a list of possibilities, you'll need to pare it down into a short list of specific goals. What should go into that list? Consider six key criteria as you decide: *personal factors, ideals, feasibility, flexibility, time,* and *priorities.* Make each of your own goals "qualify" in terms of those six criteria.

Personal Factors

As you evaluate your specific goals for assertive growth, use your discoveries about yourself from the *Assertiveness Inventory* in chapter 3 and your log entries.

A BEHAVIORAL MODEL FOR PERSONAL GROWTH
Robert E. Alberti, Ph.D.

Dr. Carl Rogers, in his book *On Becoming a Person*, identified three major characteristics of healthy personal growth. The following "behavioral model" is based on the three qualities identified by Rogers.

"An Increasing Openness to Experience"

How recently have you

❖ participated in a new sport or game?

❖ changed your views on an important (political, personal, professional) issue?

❖ tried a new hobby or craft?

❖ taken a course in a new field?

❖ studied a new language or culture?

❖ spent fifteen minutes or more paying attention to your body feelings, senses (relaxation, tension, sensuality)?

❖ listened for fifteen minutes or more to a religious, political, professional, or personal viewpoint with which you disagreed?

❖ tasted a new food, smelled a new odor, listened to a new sound?

❖ allowed yourself to cry? or to say "I care about you"? or to laugh until you cried? or to scream at the top of your lung capacity? or to admit you were afraid?

❖ watched the sun (or moon) rise or set? or a bird soar on the wind's currents? or a flower open to the sun?

❖ traveled to a place you had never been before?

❖ made a new friend? or cultivated an old friendship?

❖ spent an hour or more really communicating (actively listening and responding honestly) with a person of a different cultural or racial background?

❖ taken a "fantasy trip" — allowing your imagination to run freely for ten minutes to an hour or more?

"Increasingly Existential Living"

How recently have you

❖ done something you felt like doing at that moment, without regard for the consequences?

❖ stopped to "listen" to what was going on inside you?

❖ spontaneously expressed a feeling — anger, joy, fear, sadness, caring — without thinking about it?

❖ done what you wanted to, instead of what you thought you "should" do?

❖ allowed yourself to spend time or money on an immediate payoff rather than saving for tomorrow?

❖ bought something you wanted on impulse?

❖ done something no one (including you) expected you to do?

"An Increasing Trust in One's Organism"

How recently have you

❖ done what felt right to you, against the advice of others?

❖ allowed yourself to experiment creatively with new approaches to old problems?

❖ expressed an unpopular opinion assertively in the face of majority opposition?

❖ used your own intellectual reasoning ability to work out a solution to a difficult problem?

❖ made a decision and acted upon it right away?

❖ acknowledged by your actions that you can direct your own life?

❖ cared enough about yourself to get a physical exam (within two years)?

❖ told others of your religious faith, or philosophy of life?

❖ assumed a position of leadership in your profession, or an organization, or your community?

❖ asserted your feelings when you were treated unfairly?

❖ risked sharing your personal feelings with another person?

❖ designed and/or built something on your own?

❖ admitted you were wrong?

In chapter 4, "Keep Track of Your Growth," we suggested that you keep track of your assertive behavior using five categories:

❖ *Situations* that are difficult or easy for you.

❖ Key *people* in your life.

❖ Your *attitudes, thoughts, and beliefs* about expressing yourself.

❖ *Obstacles* to your assertiveness, such as certain people or fears.

❖ The *skills* you possess relating to assertive behavior, such as eye contact, voice volume, gestures.

Spend some time now reviewing your log, looking for ideas which will help you to define goals for yourself.

You may, for example, find a pattern of difficulty dealing with a co-worker who is pushy. Maybe she insists on doing things her way, doesn't listen to your ideas, ignores your good suggestions. Your response may be to withdraw, avoiding confrontation by swallowing your disagreement and keeping quiet. You may also be wasting time and energy as you look for ways to stay clear of her and work on your own. Could an assertive approach help you here?

Ideals

There are probably many people you admire. If you select the qualities of one or more "models" of assertiveness as ideals toward which you can strive, you'll have some specific behavioral goals already in mind. A well-chosen ideal will inspire you to stick to your goals.

A good model may be a best friend, a beloved teacher, a public figure, a community leader, an entertainer or actor, a family member, a clergyperson, a business executive, or someone of historical importance. This person's behavior can be one basis for your goals.

Focus on the qualities that you want to attain. Key in on such areas as self-confidence, courage, persistence, honesty. Measure your behavior against the model you choose.

Think often about the person. Let your reflection on your model's behavior give you energy to keep at your own process of improvement in assertiveness.

You can go a long way toward clarifying your feelings in a situation by identifying your general life goals.

Feasibility

As we have suggested at various points in *Your Perfect Right*, go after your changes in assertive behavior slowly and in small steps to increase your chances of success. Don't set your goals too high and risk early failure. Instead, do a little each day, advancing step by step.

Author/philosopher Morton Hunt illustrates this advice in a poignant way. He tells the story of how he learned to cope with major life stresses by remembering a harrowing experience at age eight. Hunt and several friends climbed a cliff near his home. Half-way up, he got very scared and could go no further. He was caught: to think of going either up or down overwhelmed him. The others left him behind as darkness approached.

Eventually his father came to the rescue, but Morton had to do the work! His father talked him down, and the pattern was established to overcome future fearfulness. The advice was timeless . . . "take one step at a time," "go inch by inch," "don't worry about what comes next," "don't look way ahead."

Later in life, when faced with major fearful events, Morton Hunt remembered that simple lesson: don't look at the dire consequences; start with the first small step and let that small success provide the courage to take another and another. The small-step goals will add up until the major goal is accomplished.

The suggestions Hunt's father gave are an excellent approach to growth in assertiveness.

Continually remind yourself to break your major goals into small, manageable steps. Take your time.

Soon the end will be in sight; you will notice changes in yourself. And you will reach your goals, one step at a time.

Flexibility

Deciding whether and how you'd like to change can be a complex and never-ending process. Goals are never "set"; they constantly change as you and your life circumstances change.

Maybe at one time you wanted to finish school, and when you did, suddenly a whole new range of possibilities opened up. Or perhaps you sought to make $20,000 a year; by the time you reached that level you needed $40,000! Then there was that promotion; when you got it, you found you didn't like your new responsibilities as well as your old.

So *change* itself is the constant factor.

Keep your goals flexible enough that you can adapt to the inevitable changes which will come in your life.

Time

How about listing your goals according to how long it will take to accomplish them? Here are some examples of assertiveness goals:

One Month Goals
❖ Return the faulty vacuum cleaner to the store.
❖ Say no to the finder of committee members at work.
❖ Get firmer in disciplining my children.
❖ Invite my new neighbor over for coffee.
❖ Start listening to audio tapes on assertiveness.

One Year Goals
❖ Compliment those close to me more frequently.
❖ Speak out in front of groups more often.
❖ Say no and stick to it!
❖ Improve my eye contact in conversation.
❖ Don't say "I'm sorry" or, "I hate to bother you" so much.

Long Range Goals
❖ Behave more assertively with my spouse.
❖ Take more risks in my life.
❖ Reduce my anxiety about behaving assertively.

❖ Overcome my fear of conflict and anger.
❖ Gain a good understanding of how my childhood experiences influenced my assertiveness.

These lists are only ideas from hundreds — or thousands — of
possibilities! Develop your own unique, personal lists. Be
assertive! No one knows your needs better than you.

Priorities

After identifying your short-range, mid-range, and long-range
lists of goals, sort each group according to your own priorities.
Identify "top, middle and bottom drawer" goals.

Top Drawer — goals which are most important.

Middle Drawer — goals which are important, but don't need to
be accomplished right away.

Bottom Drawer — those goals which can be put off indefinitely
without causing great stress.

If you'll select two top-drawer goals from each of the three time
lists, you'll have six top-priority items to work on during a period
of one month. Each month you can select a new list. Some goals
will stay top-drawer, others won't.

	One month	One year	Long range
Top drawer	• Return faulty vacuum • Invite new neighbor over	• Speak out more • Say no & stick to it! And don't say I'm sorry!	• Overcome my fear of conflict & anger • Take more risks
Middle drawer	• Start assertiveness tapes • Get firmer with kids • Say no to fund drive	• Compliment John more often	• Behave more assertively with John
Bottom drawer		• Improve eye contact	• Think about how childhood experiences influenced me

Goal for It!

You have identified some possible goals for your growth, evaluated them, and begun to sort them according to their importance and feasibility.

Select — and write in your log — a few goals to work on over the next weeks and months.

Throw out the ideas that are too far-fetched or out of reach for you at this time. Be practical at this point. Narrow down exactly what your next steps will be in your assertiveness journey.

As you proceed in your choice-making process, keep in mind your model/ideal person. See if your choices generally agree with those qualities you want to develop. Your assertive behavior won't exactly match that of your ideal — in fact, you don't want it to. You are trying to be the person *you* really are, not someone else.

Remember that your choices are always tentative and subject to change with new circumstances and information. Stay on your course, but remain flexible, making adjustments as needed. Setting goals for your own life can be an exciting process. As you take steps toward each goal, you'll find a genuine sense of accomplishment in your progress. Pat yourself on the back as you achieve each step. Use your log regularly to keep track. And most important: *let this be for you.* Your goals needn't please anybody else. Pay careful attention to your own desires and needs; *play your own game.*

Thinking Assertively

If a person continues to see only giants,
it means he is still looking at the world
through the eyes of a child.
— ANAIS NIN

OK, YOU SAY. "Maybe I'm not as assertive as I'd like to be. You can't teach an old dog new tricks. That's just the way I am. I can't change it."

We don't agree. Hundreds of thousands – perhaps millions — of people have found that it is possible to change. Becoming more assertive is a learning process, and it takes longer for some of us. But the process is not really that difficult, and the rewards are great.

Right *thinking* about assertiveness is crucial. Thoughts, beliefs, attitudes, and feelings set the stage for behavior. Your mind needs to be free to respond to each new situation calling for assertive action. Negative or faulty attitudes, beliefs, and thoughts hold you back and stop your natural flow. "You are what you think" (even more than "what you eat"). Getting your thinking straight will be a great resource to help you generate greater assertiveness. Start today to rid yourself of self-defeating thinking!

In this chapter, you will find some "pep talks" and some specific procedures that will help you to look at your thinking process in relation to assertiveness. Consider carefully what is said here. We are probably going to challenge some of your beliefs about how life works.

YOUR ATTITUDE TOWARD BECOMING ASSERTIVE

Perhaps you, like many folks, have experienced parents, teachers and peers, saying, "You have no right. . . ." Now we are telling you, "You have a perfect right . . .," that it is good, it is right, it is okay to assert yourself. How to deal with these conflicting messages? Trust yourself. Experiment a little. You owe it to yourself to try!

Your capacity to grow in assertiveness will be helped or hindered by your attitude. If you'll cooperate with the natural process of self-expression, you can learn to enjoy each new challenge. Don't let negative attitudes stunt your growth.

Maybe you're imagining all the "dire consequences" that may result from taking risks in your relationships. ("Oh, dear. What might happen? Maybe he'll hit me! Maybe she'll leave me!") Recognize that at times it's appropriate to ignore those excessive cautions, and take just one small step toward your goal. Life isn't likely to present you with any task you can't handle.

You can take charge of your own growth process, and guide your development in a positive, assertive direction. You'll find your attitudes can change because of your actions. And you may be surprised at the results. Positive responses from others, better feelings about yourself, and accomplishment of your goals will reward you for expressing yourself and standing up for your rights. Pay attention to these positive outcomes; they offer important support and encouragement as you practice new skills.

YOUR ATTITUDE TOWARD YOURSELF

Can you congratulate yourself when you succeed? When you fail, can you accept your foibles with honesty and laugh at yourself? Can you express the feeling of elation you get when you achieve a personal goal, such as completing a college course or a remodeling job on your home? Do you allow yourself the pleasure of feeling satisfied with a job well done? How about when you do something that makes someone else happy?

Maybe your goal in life is to be of service to others. If you don't take care of yourself, you'll have little to give to anyone else! If you continually inhibit your self-expression, you'll gradually lose your effectiveness in helping others as well. Recall that the commandment is to "Love others *as you love yourself.*" How well do you love yourself? Remember the "Behavioral Model for Personal Growth" in chapter 8? Read it over again now, and consider how you can love yourself better.

Your attitude toward yourself and your behavior are in a continuous cycle. When you are down on yourself, you'll tend to act in self-denying ways. Others will see those actions and respond accordingly — as if you don't deserve much respect. When you see the way they treat you, it confirms your attitude: "I knew I wasn't worth a damn! Look how people treat me!" And the self-fulfilling cycle continues.

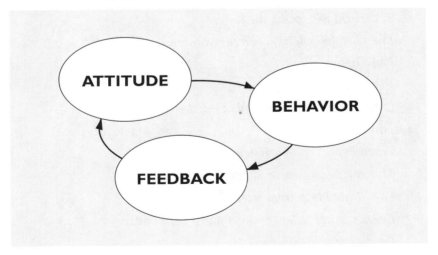

Assertiveness training breaks up the cycle by teaching you — and "authorizing" you — to behave assertively. Since you won't do it for yourself, maybe you'll do it when someone else tells you to! The trainer says, "Never mind how strange it feels, go ahead and try this new approach." When you do try it, the result is more positive feedback from other people, which in turn improves your attitude about yourself.

This enhanced sense of self-worth is the beginning of a positive turn in the attitude-behavior-feedback-attitude cycle. You can achieve the same results on your own — or perhaps with some help over the rough spots — by following the procedures described in this book. We'll get into the details of a program for behavior change a couple of chapters down the road; for now, let's take a deeper look at this business of thoughts and attitudes.

THOUGHTS THAT GET IN THE WAY OF SELF-ASSERTION

There are some patterns of thinking — both nonassertive and aggressive — which are common obstacles to assertiveness. If you're like most folks, you've heard yourself saying things like these — at least once in a while:

I'm a failure.

The world is treating me badly.

I'm a helpless victim of circumstances.

Nobody loves me.

Everybody is judging me.

Other people are in control of my destiny.

Or, on the other side:

When I speak, people listen (or else!).

The world owes me obedience.

I don't need help from anybody.

I'm not going to let them get away with that!

People are no damn good.

All of these ideas are false. (A few of them may be partly true in your life: you — and everybody else — will fail sometimes. And the world does sometimes treat us badly. And some of us are self-sufficient some of the time.)

The big problem with this kind of thinking is that you may begin to believe it. Distorted views of what's happening in your life may result from a number of circumstances. Sometimes bad events occur coincidentally and create an impression that life has it in for you. That idea can stick in your head and become a "self-fulfilling prophecy."

Most of us don't experience life as a devastating series of downers, but we all have days (and weeks!) which can bring us down on ourselves — at least for a while. Cognitive psychiatrist Aaron Beck has outlined some of the steps that commonly occur:

❖ *a predisposition to think poorly of yourself.* Maybe you have been out of a job for a while, or you did poorly in school, or you broke up a romance. Or perhaps you have a rather low opinion of yourself (self-concept). In any case, you are prepared to assume that whatever goes wrong, you're to blame.

❖ *a tendency to exaggerate problems.* Minor emergencies often seem catastrophic at the time. In the total scheme of things, however, most life situations are less critical than we assume.

❖ *an egocentric view of life events.* "Everything happens to me!" is the theme of this step. An objective view would tell a different story, but the victim sees everything that goes awry to be aimed at him or her.

❖ *a belief that life is either one way or the other.* This notion of good-bad, black-white, yes-no, limits your choices markedly. The fact is that there are a number of alternatives in most life situations.

❖ *a view of oneself as helpless or vulnerable.* "How can I possibly do anything about all the problems in my life?" You can begin to deal with them effectively if you'll break them down into small enough increments.

HELPFUL AIDS FOR HANDLING THOUGHTS

A number of excellent "cognitive-behavioral" methods have been developed for dealing with your thinking patterns. Three of the most effective are stress inoculation, thought-stopping, and positive self-statements.

Stress Inoculation — This type of "inoculation" not only minimizes expected stress, it can also be used on the spot to deal with stress. (Noted Canadian psychologist Donald Meichenbaum gets credit for this one.)

Assume you have a situation coming up which you know will be stressful, such as a job performance interview. Your supervisor tends to be a fast talker and not a good listener. In the past, you have become very uptight and upset.

To inoculate yourself this time, start by writing yourself a message about the situation beforehand. Speak to yourself as a wise counselor would. Here is a sample message:

> *"When you have your performance evaluation, relax. Don't let yourself be thrown off. It does no good to get upset. Remember your supervisor's style, and be ready for it. When your supervisor says something you question, be firm but polite in asking about it. Ask for time to consider further. Speak up about information the supervisor is forgetting. Be ready to list your accomplishments. You can handle this. Take a deep breath once in a while. You'll be fine. If surprises come, just roll with them. This is only one small event in your total life."*

Once you have a tailor-made message, read it aloud several times before the actual situation arises. Read it especially when you start worrying excessively or when you feel undue anxiety.

Remember the essence of the message so you can repeat key portions silently during the actual event (e.g., interview). If you find yourself slipping back in confidence, listen within yourself for the key parts.

One of our clients used this method successfully with her estranged husband. They were to meet in court and Letitia knew she would fall apart and perhaps ruin her chances for a fair settlement. She developed a stress inoculation message and practiced it often. When she entered the courtroom, her husband came up and said "Hi," and Letitia immediately broke into tears and ran to the bathroom! While there, she re-read her message aloud several times, regained her confidence and "sailed through" both talking to him again and the subsequent proceedings. Afterwards, she was amazed that it worked! In the past, she would have continued to be upset and cry. Stress inoculation helped Letitia through a very emotional event.

Thought Stopping — Have you ever had an annoying tune or thought continually "run through your head?" Nothing you do seems to work to stop it. That's the time to try "thought stopping," another method developed by psychiatrist Joseph Wolpe. Close your eyes right now and conjure up some recurring thought that bothers you. When it comes in clearly, yell "STOP!" out loud. (Make sure no one is nearby or they may think you a bit bizarre!) Your thoughts *will* actually stop. When they do, shift immediately to a pleasant thought to replace the unwanted one. The unwanted thought will typically return in short order, but if you will persistently repeat the procedure, it will be longer and longer before the offender sneaks back in. Soon, the unwanted thought will give up.

No, you don't have to run around yelling "STOP!" continually! The technique works just as effectively when done silently in your head. Of course, you may still want to yell it out loud once in a while because it is so much fun!

One warning: Be careful that the unwanted thoughts are not actually carrying constructive messages that you're not catching on to. You need to pay attention to *some* unpleasant thoughts and act upon them! With practice and trial and error, however, the difference between good and not-so-good thoughts will become apparent.

Positive Self-Statements — "The hardest step for most people I know," commented high school counselor Gail Wainwright at an AT group meeting, "is to *be assertive with yourself:* to convince yourself to go ahead and take the action you know is needed!"

If your thoughts are filled with self-denying "rules" and "attitudes," your behavior will in all likelihood be similar. You may think in negative statements: "I'm not important." "My opinions don't count." "No one will be interested in what I have to say." "I'll probably make a fool of myself if I say anything." "I'm really not sure." "I have no right to say that." If so, chances are very good you will act accordingly — that is, you'll keep quiet and let others control the situation!

Try, for a short period of time, to allow yourself to say the *positive* form of those statements: "I am important." "My opinions count." "Someone will be interested in what I have to say." "I have a right to say that." You don't have to act on any of these at this point, just get the feel of saying positive things to yourself. The positive self-statements procedure simply consists of developing complimentary statements about yourself that you memorize and repeat regularly. The purpose is to build self-confidence. Examples:

I am respected and admired by my friends.

I am a kind and loving person.

I have a job.

I handle anger well.

I got through school successfully.

I am firm when the situation calls for it.

Some of the statements you choose may not be totally true of you, but we want you to "fudge" a little at first. (Don't go to extremes, however. We don't agree with those who would have you go around saying "I am rich and beautiful." Unless, of course, it's true.) Then proceed as if they were true. Place these statements on the refrigerator, on the bathroom wall, in your purse or wallet. Regularly remind yourself that you are a positive and valuable person.

Positive self-statements can be used as replacement thoughts in conjunction with thought stopping. Or, they can be part of your stress inoculation message.

After you have practiced the positive thoughts for a while, you may wish to begin — still in your own thoughts — to consider the ways you would act in those situations if you followed through on the thoughts. Perhaps, for example, you were thinking, "Someone will be interested in what I have to say," in regard to joining in on a group discussion. If you were to imagine *acting* on that thought, you might see yourself asking a question of one of the more outspoken participants. Or, maybe you could just start out by saying, "I agree."

Think about ways you could *act* like a person who *thinks* positively!

STOP IMAGINING THE WORST!

Too often people do not respond assertively because they have conjured up dire consequences. "If I do this, she'll be mad." "I could never say that because he'd fire me." "I'll feel guilty." "She'll divorce me." "My mother always cries." "I'd hurt him too much." On and on go the imagined disasters. A part of the mind seems to work overtime to stifle self-expression.

Psychologist Albert Ellis calls this "catastrophisizing," and he has done a remarkable job of pointing out how such irrational beliefs hurt our chances of handling life situations well. In his book, *Feeling Better, Getting Better, Staying Better,* Ellis suggests that our thoughts always come before our emotional reactions to situations. Ellis describes some of the irrational ideas and beliefs about how life "ought to be" that lead to upsetting emotions, thus blocking adequate responses. These beliefs relate to such life events as rejection, fear, being treated unfairly. Read Ellis's book, and stop inhibiting your assertiveness by believing (irrationally) that the world should somehow be perfect!

"What Else Can I Do about My Thoughts?"

UCLA psychologist Gary Emery is another highly regarded specialist in cognitive therapy procedures. He has described a number of effective strategies and techniques for those who wish to make changes in their thinking patterns and "internal conversations."

You may find one or several of the procedures of help:

❖ *get to know and be aware of yourself.* A continuing quest for greater self awareness — your goals, dreams, feelings, attitudes, beliefs, limitations, problems — will give you a solid foundation for your self-improvement efforts.

❖ *recognize and keep track of your "automatic thoughts."* This term is used to describe the involuntary inner dialogue you experience when you face a stressful situation (e.g. "Oh dear, this is going to be . . .").

❖ *ask yourself questions to clarify your reactions to an event.* Is there good evidence for your assumptions? How logical is your reaction? Could you be oversimplifying things? Exaggerating? Taking the situation out of context?

❖ *consider possible alternative explanations.* Look at the situation from another viewpoint. Modify one fact at a time and see what happens.

❖ *ask yourself, "So what?"* Does it really matter? Even if the situation is actually as bad as you suspect, will the consequences be lasting? Will anybody really be hurt?

❖ *try to substitute positive images.* See if you can come up with a "silver lining." Might the bad news contain (or hide) some good news?

❖ *identify the payoffs for you.* Are you getting some reward for feeling bad? More attention, perhaps? Special help? Excused from work or school? Might there be an even better payoff for changing your outlook?

❖ *what if it really does happen?* What's the worst outcome likely to bring? Can you act for a while as if the feared event had already happened? Is it really as bad as you thought?

❖ *do some very specific "homework" to change your thoughts.* Go back to the previous section and develop a plan for positive self-statements, or stress inoculation, or thought stopping. Write your plan in your log, then do your homework!

ARE SOME MORE EQUAL THAN OTHERS?

One of our most important goals for this book is to help you recognize that you are *equal* to others on a human-to-human level. True, there will always be someone more talented, more assertive, more beautiful, more powerful, more wealthy, more educated. . . . But you are just as good, just as valuable, just as important *as anyone else as a human being*. That's a terribly important idea. If you want to read more about it, try the Constitition of the United States, or the United Nations *Universal Declaration of Human Rights*, or the *Bible*, or the *Koran*, or the writings of Confucius, or. . . .

10

There's Nothing to Be Afraid Of

Courage is resistance to fear,
mastery of fear, not absence of fear.
— MARK TWAIN

M ANY READERS OF *Your Perfect Right* — perhaps you, too — find anxiety to be the most significant obstacle to greater assertiveness. "Sure," you say, "I know *how* to express myself! I just get really uptight about doing it. The risks seem too great. I want people to like me. . . ."

Perhaps you find yourself perspiring, your heart racing, your hands icy, as you walk into a job interview. Or maybe you have avoided asking your boss for a raise because you fear the words will catch in your throat. Do you take the long way home so you don't have to confront the neighbor who is always asking favors that you're afraid to refuse?

You may not even be aware of the source of such fears. Often, they result from childhood experiences — for example, well-meaning parents may have taught you to "speak only when spoken to."

Although learning to be assertive will help to reduce such fears, when the level of anxiety is very high it may be necessary to deal more directly with the anxiety itself. To overcome fear, nervousness, anxiety and stress about assertiveness, it is necessary to determine what *causes* the reaction. Once you know what you are dealing with, you can learn methods to eliminate the fear.

We suggest you begin by *tracing* your fear. Narrow down exactly what causes you to feel afraid to express yourself assertively. Use your log to record your reactions systematically. Learn to keep track of what is causing your anxiety (fear) level to rise. The following section will help you to be more effective in learning about your anxiety.

FINDING YOUR FEARS: THE SUD SCALE

A useful aid in assessing your own anxiety level is the "SUD scale." "SUD" is an acronym for *subjective units of disturbance* — simply a way of rating your own physical feelings of anxiety on a scale of 0-100. SUD is an important contribution of the work of the late psychiatrist Dr. Joseph Wolpe (1969).

Because anxiety has physical elements, you can become aware of your degree of discomfort in a situation by "tuning in" to your body's indicators: heart rate (pulse), breathing rate, coldness in hands and feet, perspiration (particularly in hands), and muscle tension. (There are others, but most of us usually are not aware of them. *Biofeedback training* — electromechanical measurement and reporting of specific bodily functions, such as heart rate, skin conductivity, muscle tension, breathing — is sometimes used to allow people to learn when they are relaxed or anxious, since it offers an automatic monitor of physical indicators.)

Try this: get yourself as relaxed as you can right now — lie flat on the couch or floor or relax in your chair, breathe deeply, relax all the muscles in your body, and imagine a very relaxing scene (lying on the beach, floating on a cloud). Allow yourself to relax in this way for at least five minutes, paying attention to your heartbeat, breathing, hand temperature and dryness, muscle relaxation. Those relaxed feelings can be given a SUD scale value of 0, to represent near-total relaxation. If you did not do the relaxation exercise, but are reading this alone, relatively quietly and comfortably, you may consider yourself somewhere around 20 on the SUD scale.

At the opposite end of the scale, visualize the most frightening scene you can imagine. With your eyes closed, picture yourself narrowly escaping an accident, or being near the center of an earthquake or flood. Pay attention to the same body signals: heart rate/pulse, breathing, hand temperature/moisture, muscle relaxation. These fearful feelings can be given a SUD scale value of 100 — almost totally anxious.

Now you have a roughly calibrated comfort/discomfort scale which you can use to help yourself evaluate just how anxious you are in any given situation. Each 10 points on the scale represents a "just noticeable difference" up or down from the units above and below. Thus, 70 is slightly more anxious than 60, and by the same amount more comfortable than 80. (The SUD scale is too subjective to be able to define more closely than 10 units.)

Most of us function normally in the range of 20-50 SUDs. A few life situations will raise anxiety above 50 for short periods, and on rare occasions (rare for most of us, anyway!) one can relax below 20.

The SUD scale can help you to identify those life situations that are most troublesome. Once again, being systematic in your observations of yourself can pay big dividends! The procedure described below shows a way to use the SUD scale to develop a "plan of attack" against your fears.

List/Group/Label

A method developed in the field of creative writing will be helpful. In her book, *Project Write*, Patsy Tanabe-Endsley tells how to *list*, *group*, and *label* ideas. We can use her system by substituting "fears or anxieties" for "ideas."

Start by recording or *listing* life situations when you feel fear or anxiety. Use some space in your log to list all your reactions that hinder your assertiveness, including the situation or event involved, people, circumstances, other factors that contributed to your reaction. Assign a SUD value, as described in the previous section, to each of the items on your list.

Once you know what you are dealing with, you can learn methods to eliminate the fear.

Next, find the reactions on your list that are similar, those that seem to have a common theme, and *group* them together. Now see if you can *label* your groups, applying appropriate names to each grouping of anxiety-producing factors. Among your groups may be such common phobias as fears of snakes or spiders or heights or enclosed places. Interpersonal fears are more likely to be the problem in assertiveness. Fears of criticism, rejection, anger or aggression, or hurting the feelings of others greatly hinder your assertive response.

You may find a grouping that centers around one or more of the situations given in the *Assertiveness Inventory*. Instead of a classic fear like rejection, you may simply experience a good deal of anxiety when standing in line or when facing salespersons. Perhaps people in authority scare you. Obviously, your assertiveness will not be optimum if your anxiety is already working against you beforehand!

Now, one more step in this analysis of your fears. In each labeled group, re-list the items in order, according to the SUD scores you have assigned. Now you have a rough agenda, in priority order, for dealing with your anxieties! Usually it is best to start working to reduce or overcome those which are most disturbing before you attempt to develop your assertive skills further.

The sample log entries on the next page will help make this process clearer.

September 13, 2002

Today I'm going to write down situations when I feel anxious, including a "SUDs" estimate. I want to try the "list, group, label" method to see if I can figure out any patterns of fears.

1. Magazine article about open-heart surgery made me nauseous.   SUDs 50

2. I was upset when Jose ignored me at lunch.   SUDs 30

3. The boss looked disgusted when I made
    several mistakes at work.   SUDs 65

4. Elise told me she talked with Connie (ex-wife) about the kids.

    I was so angry that Connie criticized my discipline.   SUDs 80!

5. Roommate didn't help with the dishes.   SUDs 55

6. Cut my finger; seeing the blood made me queasy.   SUDs 35

7. I was embarrassed about being late to the meeting.   SUDs 25

8. Friends teased me about my new haircut.   SUDs 25

Groups	Labels
A. 2, 3, 7, 8	Being too sensitive
B. 4, 5	Anger
C. 1, 6	Medical fears

Well, if this is a typical day, looks like I'm more sensitive about criticism than I thought. Maybe I should look into that "desensitization" exercise Dr. G. told me about.

METHODS FOR OVERCOMING ANXIETY

Now that you have carefully identified the anxieties which are inhibiting your assertiveness, you will want to begin a program to overcome them. There are a number of effective approaches. Since this topic is a book in itself, let us briefly describe two popular approaches — one widely used and proven over many years; the other a recent innovation, still controversial but rapidly gaining support in research and practice — then we'll refer you to other resources for detailed information.

Systematic Desensitization

This approach, controversial and experimental when introduced thirty-plus years ago, is another that was developed by assertiveness training pioneer Joseph Wolpe. Like AT, systematic desensitization is based on learning principles; you *learned* to be anxious about expressing yourself, and you can *unlearn* it. No one was born fearful!

Practically speaking, it isn't possible to be relaxed and anxious at the same time. The process of desensitization involves repeated association of an anxiety-producing situation with a feeling of deep relaxation throughout your body. Gradually, you learn to "automatically" associate relaxation — instead of anxiety — with the situation. In a therapeutic desensitization, you first learn to relax your entire body completely through practicing a series of deep muscle relaxation exercises, or through hypnosis. The anxious situation is then presented in a series of imagined scenes, arranged in a hierarchy from least to greatest anxiety.

You are then told to imagine yourself in the least anxious scene of your hierarchy, and to be aware of the anxiety that results. After five to fifteen seconds you'll switch your visualization back to your relaxing scene, relaxing once again. This procedure is repeated several times for each step of the hierarchy of anxious scenes. The repeated exposure to your anxious scene while you are relaxed gradually reduces your fear of the stimulus scenes.

> *It is not possible*
> *to be relaxed*
> *and anxious*
> *at the same time.*

The intricacies of the procedure are somewhat more complex, but that is the essence of desensitization. It has been proven effective for a wide range of fears, including phobic reactions to heights, public speaking, animals, flying, test taking, social contact, and many more.

Eye Movement Desensitization and Reprocessing (EMDR)

This method of anxiety reduction, which shows great promise, was developed in the 1990s. It has created a good deal of commotion because it seems a bit "magical." EMDR involves moving your eyes back and forth as you remember upsetting memories concerning past traumas or anxiety-provoking situations. Shown to be helpful in overcoming the after-effects of traumatic stress situations (physical or sexual abuse, war experiences, accidents, natural disasters, dysfunctional family experiences), EMDR was discovered and developed by psychologist Francine Shapiro.

The EMDR method also appears to be effective in dealing with the anxieties and fears that often surround behaving assertively. EMDR is showing excellent results in helping overcome the guilt, fear, upset, faulty thinking, and anxiety that often result from traumatic experiences. And EMDR has also been successful in overcoming phobias like fear of confrontation, hurting others' feelings, or being the center of attention.

Some commotion has surrounded the introduction of EMDR, due to the funny "eye movement" requirement, the fact that the method often works very rapidly, and Shapiro's early demand that the method be employed only by practitioners she had personally trained. These factors, and the fact that research on the method is in the early stages, caused some controversy in the mental health community.

(Michael Emmons has been trained in EMDR therapy and has used it in his practice. He is enthusiastic about the early results and predicts that EMDR will soon gain widespread acceptance as a method for helping people overcome anxieties, fears, and traumas.)

TACKLING YOUR OWN ANXIETY

If you are very concerned about your anxiety, you may wish to do some further reading. Two good books on the topic are *The Stress Owner's Manual* by Michele Haney and Ed Boenisch (1996), and *The Anxiety and Phobia Workbook* by Edmund Bourne (1990). Both books explore self-help procedures for anxiety and describe further resources available. If you are experiencing major anxiety attacks — panic at just the thought of a confrontation, for example, or for no apparent reason at all — another excellent self-help book may be just the thing to help you deal with it: *Master Your Panic and Take Back Your Life*, by Wisconsin psychologist Denise Beckfield.

Expect to invest some time — probably several weeks — practicing your choice of the methods of anxiety relief. It took time for you to learn to be anxious; it will take time to learn to overcome it.

This discussion of anxiety about assertiveness is not meant to discourage you. On the contrary, most readers will find themselves able to handle their mild discomfort about self-expression without major difficulty. There are some of us, however, who do need some extra help in overcoming obstacles. Don't be embarrassed or hesitant about asking for help, just as you would seek competent medical aid for a physical problem. Then, when you've cleared up the anxiety obstacle, turn back to the procedures outlined in this book for developing your assertiveness.

SUMMARY

Feelings of nervousness, anxiety reactions, and fear are common when thinking about and acting assertively. Often, practicing assertive responses will reduce these uneasy reactions to manageable levels. Practice will make assertion feel more natural to you. If you feel that you are still too afraid, there are systematic ways to identify the situations that trigger fearful reactions, and to reduce the level of anxiety.

Simply understanding a fear is seldom powerful enough to reduce it significantly. Self-help methods that help eliminate or lower the fear to manageable levels are often successful. Professional therapy is recommended when your own efforts are not enough.

We've called this chapter, "There's Nothing to Be Afraid Of." Actually, life hands all of us situations we find fearful at times. What we want you to remember is that *there are effective ways to deal with anxiety*. If it's a problem for you, we urge you to read this chapter again, learn as much as you can about your anxiety, and seek out methods — including professional therapy if necessary — that will help you overcome it.

11

It's a Skill You Can Learn

Peace cannot be kept by force.
It can only be achieved
by understanding.
— ALBERT EINSTEIN

I T'S AN OLD JOKE IN PSYCHOLOGY. When two engineers (lawyers, housekeepers, plumbers, nurses) are talking together and a psychologist walks up and joins the conversation, there are now two engineers and a psychologist. But when two psychologists are talking and an engineer (substitute your own favorite) walks up and joins them, there are now three *psychologists!*

Everyone believes she/he is a psychologist in some sense. Indeed, we all have some practical first-hand knowledge of human behavior, beginning with ourselves. Unfortunately, a lot of what *seems* true is not.

CHANGING BEHAVIOR AND ATTITUDES
Popular wisdom often suggests that to improve yourself you need to "change your attitude." For many years, until late in the twentieth century, behavioral psychologists argued that it was more important to change *behavior*, that attitude change would follow.

A great deal of recent research in a field of psychology called *cognitive behavior therapy* has shown that, for many people at least, *thoughts are as important as actions* in bringing about life changes.

In the first three editions of this book, we advocated the position of traditional behavior therapy, that it is easier and more effective to change behavior first, then attitude change would slowly follow. While there is still little doubt that attitude change is the "tougher nut to crack," psychologists have learned that thoughts and beliefs can be modified by procedures such as those described in chapter 9, and that such changes will powerfully affect behavior.

Positive self-statements provide a good example. By consciously telling yourself "I have the ability to succeed in this situation," you greatly enhance your chances of success, even without any other changes. We view and interpret life events through our own unique attitudes and beliefs about ourselves and the world, and we act according to those interpretations. If I go about believing that "I am no damn good," I will approach life situations with an outlook of failure — and thus increase my chance of failure. If I tell myself I am capable of succeeding, my actions will be more likely to follow a pattern of success.

For a time, the "cognitive folks" seemed to have everyone convinced that such changed thinking was all-important. That usually happens when a new idea emerges from psychological research. Very recently, the "pendulum" has begun to swing back toward a more moderate position, and that is the view we hold: *Both thinking and behavior are vital elements in the process of bringing about personal growth.* Some people respond more readily to cognitive (thinking) interventions, others to behavioral (action) interventions. In any comprehensive program for growth, therefore, both areas must be dealt with. Put most of your energy into whichever is most helpful for you!

(Funny how psychological research catches up with common sense if we allow enough time to pass!)

GETTING THERE FROM HERE

As you begin the process of becoming more assertive, don't expect to wake up some morning and say, "Today, I'm a new, assertive person!" You will find here, spelled out in detail in the following chapter, a systematic, step-by-step guide to change. The key to developing assertiveness is *practice*.

Cycles of behavior tend to repeat, and to perpetuate themselves, until a decisive intervention occurs. People who have acted nonassertively or aggressively in relationships for a long time typically don't think much of themselves. Their behavior toward others may be inhibited or abusive — either usually is met with scorn, disdain, or avoidance. When those inevitable responses come, such a person says, "See, I knew I was no damn good!" The person is confirmed in a low self-evaluation, and the cycle is repeated: self-defeating behavior, negative feedback from others, self-critical attitude, self-defeating behavior, and so on. . . . (Remember the illustration of cycles in chapter 9?)

The cycle can be reversed, becoming a positive sequence: more appropriately assertive *behavior* gains more positive responses from others; positive feedback leads to an improved evaluation of *self-worth:* ("Wow, people are treating me like a worthwhile person!"); and improved attitudes about oneself result in further assertiveness.

Or, the cycle may be entered at the point of *thoughts:* by saying positive things to yourself and beginning to think of yourself as a valuable person, you'll begin to act more appropriately. Your more effective action will usually produce more positive responses from others and the resulting confirmation of the original thought: "Maybe I *am* a good person, after all!"

JB had been convinced for years that he was truly worthless. He was totally dependent upon his wife for emotional support and, despite a rather handsome appearance and ability to express himself well, had literally no friends. Imagine his utter despair when his wife left him! Fortunately, JB was seeing a psychologist at the time and, after several months of therapy working on recovery from his loss, he was willing to begin to make contact with other people. When his first attempts at assertiveness with eligible women were successful, the reward of this response to his assertions was very great! JB's entire outlook toward himself changed, and he became much more assertive in a variety of situations.

Not everyone, to be sure, will experience such an immediate "payoff" for assertion; and not all assertions are fully successful. Success usually requires a great deal of patience, and a gradual process of handling more and more difficult situations.

Generally speaking, *assertiveness is self-rewarding.* It feels good to have others begin to respond more attentively, to achieve your goals in relationships, to find situations going your way more often. And you can make these changes happen.

Remember, *begin with assertions where you are somewhat certain of success before proceeding to more difficult ones* requiring greater confidence and skill. It is often quite helpful and reassuring to obtain support and guidance from a friend, practice partner, teacher, or professional therapist.

Keep in mind that changed behavior leads to changed attitudes about oneself and one's impact upon people and situations. Moreover, changed thinking leads to changed behavior. The following chapter presents the steps involved in bringing about these changes. Read all the material carefully first. Then begin to follow the steps in your own life. You'll like the difference in you!

WHEN YOU ARE READY TO BEGIN

First, make certain that you understand thoroughly the basic principles of assertion. Recognizing the differences between assertive and aggressive behavior is important to your under-standing and success. Re-read chapters 2, 5 and 6 if you need to.

Second, decide whether you are ready to begin trying self-assertive behavior on your own. If you have chronic patterns of nonassertiveness or aggression or if you are highly anxious, be more cautious. We recommend slow and careful practice and work with another person, preferably a trained therapist, as a facilitator. This recommendation is particularly strong for those who feel very anxious about beginning, as we discussed in chapter 10.

Third, your initial attempts at being assertive should be chosen for their high potential of success, so as to provide reinforcement. The more successfully you assert yourself at first, the more likely you are to be successful from then on!

Begin with small assertions that are likely to be rewarding, and from there move on to more difficult situations and relationships. Be very careful about attempting a difficult assertion without special preparation. And don't instigate an assertion where you are likely to fail miserably and discourage your further attempts at assertiveness.

If you do suffer a setback, which very well may happen, take time to analyze the situation carefully and regain your confidence, getting help from a friend or facilitator if necessary. Especially in the early stages of assertion, it is not unusual to experience difficulty. You're still perfecting your technique, after all! Or you may overdo it, to the point of aggression. Either error is likely to cause a negative response, particularly if the target of your assertion becomes hostile and highly aggressive. Don't let such an occurrence stop you. Consider your goal again, and remember that although success requires lots of practice, the rewards are great.

There will be some failures. These procedures will not turn you into a 100-percent success in all your relationships! There are no instant or magic answers to life's problems. The fact is, assertiveness does not *always* work — for *us* either! Sometimes, your goals will be incompatible with the other person's. Two people can't be at the head of the same line. (Letting the other person go first can be an assertive act, too!) At times, others may be unreasonable or unyielding, and the best of assertions will be to no avail.

Also, because you're human, you'll blow it sometimes — as we all do. Allow yourself to make mistakes! And allow others their right to be themselves as well. You'll be uncomfortable, disappointed, discouraged. Reassess, practice, then try again.

The key to all of this, of course, is *choice*. If you choose to express yourself, do so, and do not succeed in gaining your goals, is that failure? We don't think so. The choice itself was an assertive act, as was the attempt. Outcomes are never guaranteed in life!

If you feel your assertions are failing a bit too often, take a close look at what's going on. Are you setting your goals too high? Take small steps to ensure success! Are you overdoing it and becoming aggressive? Monitor your behavior carefully — refer to your log and check yourself. (Some aggression may be expected at first. The pendulum will balance in a short time.)

We all want our assertions to work, and to achieve our goals. Nevertheless, the greatest value of self-assertion is the good feeling that comes from having expressed yourself. To know that *you have a perfect right to self-expression,* and to feel free to say what you're feeling are the best benefits of all.

Usually, you'll find assertiveness will make things happen. But whether it works or not, remember how good it felt to speak up for yourself! You did what you could, even if the outcome wasn't what you hoped for. If you have genuinely tried and done all you can, that's all you can ask of yourself!

One final caution: Nothing turns people off faster than a self-righteous attitude. Avoid the trap some new assertiveness trainees fall into — feeling you *must* assert yourself in all situations, at all costs. Let moderation, consideration for others, and common sense prevail! (More on this in chapter 20.)

Ready to move ahead? Chapter 12 shows how — step by step.

12

Take It One Step at a Time

Believe in life!
Always human beings will live and progress
to greater, broader, and fuller life.
— W. E. B. DuBois

THE STEP-BY-STEP PROCESS
FOR INCREASING YOUR ASSERTIVENESS

Step 1. Observe your own behavior. Are you satisfied with your effectiveness in interpersonal relationships? Are you asserting yourself adequately? Look over your personal log, and the discussion in chapters 1-6, and assess how you feel about yourself and your behavior.

Step 2. Keep track of your assertiveness. Keep your log very carefully for a week without trying to change the way you act. Each day, record those situations in which you found yourself responding assertively, those in which you blew it, and those you avoided altogether so you would not have to face the need to act assertively. Be honest with yourself, and systematic, following the guidelines for self-assessment described in chapters 3 and 4.

Step 3. Set realistic goals for yourself. Your self-assessment will help you select specific targets for your growth in assertiveness. Pick out situations in which, or people toward whom, you want to become more effective. Be sure to start with a small, low-risk step to maximize your chances of success. (See chapter 8.)

Step 4. Concentrate on a particular situation. Spend a few moments with your eyes closed, imagining how you handled a specific incident (being short-changed at the supermarket, having a friend "talk your ear off" on the telephone when you had too much to do, letting the boss make you feel like "two cents" over a small mistake). Imagine vividly the actual details, including your specific feelings at the time and afterward. Appendix A offers many sample situations for your practice.

Step 5. Review your responses. Get out your log and write down your behavior in Step 4. Make use of the components of assertiveness noted in chapter 7 (eye contact, body posture, gestures, facial expression, voice, message content, etc.). Look carefully at the components of your behavior in the recalled incident, including your thoughts. Note your strengths. Be aware of those components that represent nonassertive or aggressive behavior. If a major element of your response involves anxiety, refer to the discussion in chapter 10. Do not attempt to force yourself into very painful situations. On the other hand, do not avoid new growth if it is only moderately uncomfortable!

Step 6. Observe an effective model. At this point it would be very helpful to watch someone who handles the same situation very well. Again, watch for the components discussed in chapter 7, particularly the *style* — the words are less important. If the model is a friend, discuss his/her approach, and its consequences.

Step 7. Consider alternative responses. What are other possible ways the incident could be handled? Could you deal with it more directly? More firmly? Less offensively? Refer to the chart in chapter 5, and differentiate among nonassertive, aggressive, and assertive responses.

Step 8. Imagine yourself handling the situation. Close your eyes and visualize yourself dealing effectively with your practice situation. You may act similarly to the model you observed in Step 6, or in a very different way. Be assertive, but be as much your natural self as you can. Develop strategies or ways of coping with blocks in your visualization. If you notice yourself feeling anxious, calm yourself. If negative thoughts interrupt your assertion, replace them with positive statements. Self-correct as you proceed. Cope with disruptions of your assertive response in your visualization. Repeat this step as often as necessary until you can imagine yourself handling the situation well.

Step 9. Practice positive thoughts. Spend some time going over the material in chapter 9. Develop a list of several brief positive statements about yourself that are related to this situation (e.g., "I've had job interviews before, and have done alright"). Practice saying those statements to yourself several times. Remember, this is not a "script" for what to say to someone else, it is a "prompter" for what to say to yourself.

Step 10. Get help if you need it. As we have noted before, the process of becoming more assertive may require you to stretch yourself considerably. If you feel unable on your own to deal with the situations you have visualized, seek help from a qualified professional.

Step 11. Try it out. You have examined your own behavior, considered alternatives, observed a model of more adaptive action, and practiced some positive thoughts about yourself. You are now prepared to begin trying out for yourself new ways of dealing with the problem situation. A repeat of Steps 6, 7, 8 and 9 may be needed until you are ready to proceed. It is important to select an alternative, more effective way of behaving in the problem situation. You may wish to follow your model and enact the same approach. Such a choice is appropriate, but should reflect an awareness that you are a unique person. You may not find the model's approach one which you want to adopt for yourself.

After selecting a more effective alternative behavior, role-play the situation with a friend, practice partner, teacher, or therapist. Try to follow the new response pattern you have selected. As in

Steps 2, 4, and 5, make careful observation of your behavior, using audio or videotape whenever possible. Don't worry about not having your goals absolutely clear. As you try out new behavioral skills, you'll become more aware of what you want in the situation.

Step 12. Get feedback. This step essentially repeats Step 5 with emphasis on the positive aspects of your behavior. Note particularly the strengths of your performance, and go to work on your weaker areas.

Step 13. Shape your behavior. Repeat Steps 8, 9, 11 and 12 as often as you find it helpful to "shape" your behavior — by this process of successive approximations of your goal — until you feel satisfied that you're able to deal with the situation effectively.

Step 14. Give yourself a "real world" test. You are now ready to give your new response pattern a real test. Up to this point your preparation has taken place in a relatively secure environment. Nevertheless, careful training and repeated practice have prepared you to react almost automatically. You should be ready to proceed with an actual trial. If you are unwilling to do so, further rehearsals or help may be needed. (Repeat steps 8-12). Moving from intention to action — being assertive with yourself — may be the most important step of all!

Step 15. Evaluate the test. Make notes in your log to record how your "real world" trial(s) go. Note the overall result, your general impressions of your effectiveness, your SUDs level (chapter 10), and details on the specific components of your behavior (chapter 7). If a friend observed you, get feedback from him or her. If you used a micro-cassette recorder to tape your verbal effectiveness, listen to the tape. This step is an important part of the learning process. Don't ignore it!

Step 16. Continue your training. Repeat the procedures that help you develop your desired behaviors for other specific situations which have given you trouble. Look over chapter 6 and Appendix A for examples which may be helpful in planning your own program for change.

Step 17. Set up "social reinforcement." As a final step in establishing an independent behavior pattern, it is very important that you understand the need for on-going support and rewards. In order to maintain your new assertive skills, set up a system of rewards in your own environment. For example, you now know the good feeling that comes from a successful assertion and you can rest assured that this good response will continue. Admiration from others will be another continuing positive response to your growth. Write down in your log a personal checklist of specific reinforcements — rewarding results — which are unique to your own environment and relationships.

We have spelled out this step-by-step process in detail because we know it works. Although we emphasize the importance of systematic procedures, we recommend you take into account your own personal needs, objectives, and learning style. Create a learning environment which will help you grow in assertiveness. No one system is right for everyone.

A number of approaches to assertiveness training have proved valuable, and you may wish to explore materials noted in the Bibliography for other important contributions to AT practice.

There is, of course, no substitute for active practice of assertive thoughts and behavior in your own life, when you choose to, as a means of developing greater assertiveness and enjoying its rewards.

In the chapters that follow, you'll find many ideas for developing and applying your growing assertiveness. We urge you to keep at it, and to apply the principles and procedures you've learned — at least a little every day.

*The Step-by-Step
Process for Increasing
Your Assertiveness*

17. Set up "social reinforcement"

16. Continue your training

15. Evaluate the test

14. Give yourself a "real world" test

13. Shape your behavior

12. Get feedback

11. Try it out

10. Get help if you need it

9. Practice positive thoughts

8. Imagine yourself handling the situation

7. Consider alternative responses

6. Observe an effective model

5. Review your responses

4. Concentrate on a particular situation

3. Set realistic goals for yourself

2. Keep track of your assertiveness

1. Observe your own behavior

Part IV

Applying Your Assertivenes

Assertiveness Builds Equal Relationships

Unity is plural and, at minimum, is two.
— R. BUCKMINSTER FULLER

"STAND UP FOR YOURSELF" is the slogan often equated with being assertive. But there's much more to assertive living than defending your rights. We've observed that positive, caring feelings are more difficult for many people to express than "standing up for yourself" behavior. Expressions of warmth are often held back, particularly by adults. Embarrassment, fear of rejection or ridicule, the idea that reason is superior to emotion — all are excuses for not expressing warmth, caring, and love spontaneously.

Even "thank you" is difficult for some people. Geoffrey, CEO of an organization with thousands of employees, rarely expressed appreciation directly to the people on his staff. A job well done was seldom openly rewarded, recognized, or even acknowledged. Because the chief executive was afraid to act in warm and positive ways (perhaps he might appear "soft," or others might come to *expect* rewards?), the morale of staff members in that organization was not very high.

To be a caring person, and to show it, seems to be a "high-risk" style in our society. How sad for all of us that we make it so difficult for warmth to be expressed openly! Assertiveness training can contribute much to greater freedom in communication of positive feelings toward others.

The first edition of *Your Perfect Right* was devoted almost exclusively to fostering "stand-up-for-yourself" behavior. In a critical review of that first edition, published in the professional journal *Behavior Therapy,* the late psychiatrist Michael Serber noted our oversight. Serber, a colleague who had substantial influence on our work, wrote in that early review (1971):

> *Certainly, behavioral skills necessary to stand up to the multiple personal, social, and business situations confronting the majority of people are imperative to master. But what of other just as necessary skills, such as being able to give and take tenderness and affection? Is not the expression of affection toward other people also assertion? . . . the ability to express warmth and affection, to be able to give and take feelings, including anger, badly needs . . . special attention . . . humanistic goals and behavioral techniques can yield both meaningful and concrete new behaviors.*

In this chapter, we'll give special attention to the expression of affection.

"WHAT THE WORLD NEEDS NOW . . ."

More than four decades ago, psychoanalyst Eric Fromm defined five types of love in his excellent book *The Art of Loving.* The book is old, but Fromm's perspective on love is timeless. He discusses at length the concepts of fraternal love, maternal love, erotic love, love of God, and self-love.

Fraternal love, for example — caring for other members of the human family — is a very different quality than the popular romantic idea of "love." It is a vital and critically important aspect of our lives on this small planet. However independent we may become, we humans are fundamentally interdependent and social creatures!

Author Robert Solomon, in his book *About Love,* looks at love as "shared identity." In his view, healthy couples build the self-esteem of each partner by providing each other a sense of wholeness or completion that neither can have alone. Such couples are engaged in a joint effort to bring out the best in each other, and love represents a process of mutual self-improvement. Thus love is reciprocal, equal, active, dynamic, and a process that nurtures itself: *love creates love.* Solomon is obviously an idealist, but his notions represent a worthy — and surprisingly attainable — goal for loving relationships.

Effective assertive communication can build positive, equal relationships between people — the most valuable assets any human being can have.

REACHING OUT

Expressing your warm feelings for another person is a highly assertive act. And, as with other assertions we have noted, the action itself is more important by far than the words you use. This is even more true for expressions of caring. Nothing represents a more personal, individual expression than that which says, "You mean a great deal to me at this moment."

Here are some ways of communicating that message:

❖ A warm, firm, and extended handshake.

❖ A hug, the squeeze of an arm, an arm around the shoulders, an affectionate pat on the back, the squeeze of a hand held affectionately.

❖ Sincerely warm words, such as
   "Thank you."
   "You're great!"
   "I really understand what you mean."
   "I like what you did."
   "I'm here."
   "I believe you."
   "I trust you" (better yet an act of trust).
   "I love you."
   "I believe in you."

"I'm glad to see you."
"You've been on my mind."

❖ A warm smile.

❖ Extended eye contact.

❖ A gift of love (made by the giver, or uniquely special to the recipient).

None of these messages is new to you. Yet you may find it difficult to allow yourself to do or say them. It is too easy to be hung up on embarrassment, or to assume: "She knows how I feel," or "He doesn't care to hear that." But who doesn't care to hear that? All of us need to know we are cared about and admired and needed. If those around us are too subtle in their expressions of positive regard, we may begin to doubt, and perhaps to look elsewhere for human warmth.

We asked a group of university students to tell what makes each of them feel especially good. Some of their favorite experiences are in the following list (notice how many involve someone else caring!):

Acceptance of my invitation	Jobs completed
Achievement	Keeping my plants alive
Affection	Laughter
Approval	Making new friends
Assurance	My boyfriend's/girlfriend's actions of love
Compliments from the opposite sex	toward me
Encouragement	Personal satisfaction with myself
Expressed interest of another	Positive comment
Friendliness	Praise
Getting an A on an exam	Receiving a compliment
Giving a compliment	Recognition
Good grades	Recognition when speaking
Greeting someone else	Request to repeat a job previously done
Having a friend	Satisfaction
Having someone say "hello"	Security
Helping others	Singing
Implementation of ideas	Spoken affirmation
Independence	Touch

We all need positive contacts with others. Therapists encounter many, many clients who are unhappy precisely because they are not getting such "strokes" in their lives.

Imagine the following scenes:

. . . While you are wandering alone at a large gathering, a stranger walks up to you and starts a conversation, and you no longer feel anxious and lost.

. . . Three days after you arrive in a new neighborhood, the couple next door come to welcome you with a pot of coffee and a freshly baked cake.

. . . During your visit in another country, you are looking in vain for a street sign. A native appears and asks, "May I help you find something?"

Take a few moments to jot down in your log how you would feel in each of those situations.

Thoughtful acts like these are not only strokes for the receiver, they produce warm feelings for the person who reached out assertively. People often hesitate to initiate contact in these ways for fear of rejection — a common excuse for avoiding assertions! Such initiative involves concern for the other person, and some courage of your own. Yet, realistically, who could reject such a kindness?

Often actions like these are easier than you might suppose. As you enter a classroom, a meeting, or a bus, think how easy it would be simply to approach a vacant seat and ask the person sitting nearest, "Is anyone sitting here?" Not only have you found a place to sit — assuming the seat is available — *you have begun a conversation!* Having thus opened contact, you may easily proceed to find out more about the other person: "Where are you headed?" "Have you heard this lecturer before?" "My name is . . ."

Don't wait for others to take the initiative. Take the risk of reaching out! It's a key means of caring about yourself and about others, and an important step toward greater assertiveness and more fun!

"Thanks, I Needed That!"

Compliments are a frequent source of discomfort on both sides, sadly enough. To praise someone as a person or to recognize something someone has done may be a difficult thing for you. Again, we encourage practice. Go out of your way to praise others — not dishonestly or insincerely, but whenever a genuine opportunity presents itself. Don't concern yourself with waiting for the right words either. Your thoughtfulness — the honest expression of what you are feeling — will convey itself, *if you act!* Try simply, "I like what you did" or "Great!" or a big smile.

Accepting compliments — receiving very supportive statements directed toward you, or about you to a third person — is perhaps an even more challenging task, particularly difficult if you are not feeling good about yourself. Nevertheless, it is an assertive act — and mutually enhancing — to accept praise from another person.

Think about it: you really have no right to deny another person's *perception* of you. If you say, "Oh, you just caught me on a good day!" or "It wasn't anything special" or "It was an accident that it turned out well," you have in effect said the complimentor has poor judgment. It is as if you told that person, "You're wrong!" Try to allow everyone the right to feelings, and if they are positive toward you, do others — and yourself — the courtesy of accepting.

You don't have to go around praising yourself, or taking credit for achievements which are not your own. However, when another person sincerely wishes to convey a positive comment about you, allow the expression, without rejection or qualification. Try saying at the least, "It's hard for me to accept that, but thank you," or better yet simply, "That feels good" or "I like to hear that."

Friendship

"Nancy has seen me at my worst, watched me make stupid mistakes, felt the sting of my unjustified anger, and been there when I was coming apart at the seams. It's amazing; she's still my friend!"

There is no relationship quite like that of friendship. Not so irrational as love; yet far more intense than acquaintance, friendship is perhaps the least understood of human interactions.

Actual *knowledge* about friendship continues to be sketchy at best; most relationship research involves strangers or lovers. Yet some popular wisdom is useful in examining the bond between friends:

> *Effective assertive communication can build positive, equal relationships between people.*

. . . Friends have some interests in common.

. . . Friends share an on-going relationship, with periodic (although not necessarily regular) contact.

. . . Friends trust one another, at least to some extent, with information, money, safety, other relationships.

. . . Friends can say "no" to each other and still remain friends.

. . . Friends can see — and accept — the worst in each other.

. . . Friends rarely feel they "owe" each other anything; give and take is without obligation between them (perhaps with some limits!).

. . . Friendship is also characterized by understanding, communication, acceptance, lack of embarrassment, trust.

Friendship is held within us, an attitude toward another person much like love, anger, or prejudice. It requires no regular outward expression. It requires merely a *feeling of commitment* to the relationship. Often such a feeling is supported by the belief that the other person cares about you, that the other values the relationship as well. If we believe that we are important to each other — important enough that we think of each other warmly now and again — we will likely remain friends, even if we don't see each other for years.

It is common to see tearful reunions at airports, parties and homecomings between friends who have not seen each other for years. Friendships often survive no more contact than an annual ritual holiday card! What keeps them going? Can such a relationship really be called a "friendship?" Why not?

"True friendship," says Letty Cottin Pogrebin in her book, *Among Friends,* "describes a feeling . . . best captured by the word 'soulmate' in Aristotle's sense of 'a single soul dwelling in two bodies' . . . a feeling that can happen to any two people who are caught up in the act of being themselves, together, and who like what they see."

But what has this to do with assertiveness? How does assertive action contribute to friendship, or vice versa?

Let us pose an unproven theory for your consideration: *If you act assertively most of the time, you are more likely to have satisfying relationships than if you act in nonassertive or aggressive ways.* We cannot prove that idea. In fact, we have not even dreamed up a research study which would allow us to test it (if you do, we would love to hear from you!). But our observation of assertive people over many years leads us to conclude that it is a pretty good bet!

Acting on that hypothesis, then, and assuming that you would like to have satisfying relationships, we invite you to apply the assertive skills you are learning to the development of friendship:

❖ Take the risks necessary to build an acquaintance into a friend.

❖ Allow yourself to be seen as you are by your friend.

❖ Share something of yourself you would not ordinarily tell someone else.

❖ Be spontaneous with your new friend, suggest an activity on the spur of the moment, really listen to what is important in your friend's life, give a gift for no special occasion.

❖ Ask your friend's advice with a problem or help with a project (remembering that an assertive friend can say "no" and still like you!).

❖ Simply tell the person you like him/her.

❖ Clear the air between you; if you are annoyed or suspect that your friend may be, bring it up.

❖ Get *honest*. Don't allow assumptions to define your relationship. If the relationship can't handle it, it probably would not have lasted anyway; if it can, you'll be miles ahead!

As adults, friendship helps to define who we are, much as family does when we are children. (The absence of friends also says a great deal about us.) Assertive action on your part can make all the difference in nurturing friendships. Maybe you've put it off long enough?

Gender Menders

One of the most obvious realms of concern about equality in relationships has been that of the "battle of the sexes." The last quarter of the twentieth century saw major changes in how we view male-female relationships — at home, at work, in society.

In times of upheaval in such ingrained social traditions as sex roles, of course, misunderstandings are abundant and stress levels are high. After all, both genders had been conditioned for generations to behave toward each other in certain ways. What's more, there are hereditary, biological, and biochemical factors that have influenced each differently. The abandonment of traditions and movement toward equality has come with a price, and each of us may choose to pay that price with impatience and conflict, or with patience and cooperation.

Sociolinguist Deborah Tannen, author of the popular bestsellers *You Just Don't Understand* and *Talking Nine to Five,* says that women and men are raised in different cultures. Tannen stops short of saying that one upbringing is more responsible for our gender acculturation than the other. There are inequalities, biases, prejudices, myths, and false beliefs within both male and female cultures, and it doesn't help anything to assume that any of us consciously sets out to cause difficulties for each other.

We suggest an assertive effort — based on patience and cooperation — to mend, not bend the gender gap:

❖ Make equality your goal.

❖ Let each gender become more aware of the characteristic attitudes, needs, and behaviors of the other. Read books like *You Just Don't Understand.*

❖ Work on your assertive communication skills, especially listening, in order to understand and explore gender differences. Remember that there are generalities about each gender, but also unique things about each person.

❖ Discuss what you can do differently in your relationships with the opposite gender to bridge the gap. Work on accepting and respecting each other.

❖ Learn about the masculine and feminine parts of yourself, so you can improve your relationship with both genders.

❖ Treat every other person with respect, regardless of gender.

PARENTS AND CHILDREN IN THE ASSERTIVE FAMILY

How long has it been since you were on a seesaw or teeter-totter? Remember how you could affect the ride of the person on the other end by shifting your weight forward or back? If you moved forward quickly, your friend would likely drop with a solid bump! By leaning way back, you could keep the other suspended in mid-air.

Families and other interpersonal systems have a balance system not unlike that of the seesaw. A change in one member of the family will generally upset the balance of the total system, affecting everyone. Often families are strong "resistors" of change because of the delicate balance in family relationships, even though the system may be painful — or even destructive.

Becoming more assertive is clearly a change that may upset the family balance.

Ellen, for example, had been a passive wife and mother for years. As she began to express a new assertiveness, severe strains were introduced into the family system. The children, previously able to manipulate her easily, had to find new and more direct avenues to achieve their goals. Reluctantly supportive, husband Joe was soon ironing his own shirts and sharing in household chores, since Ellen had gone back to school full time.

Such changes present a difficult adjustment for everyone. The prospect of such disruption of the family balance can be a considerable obstacle to the person who wishes to become more assertive. A traditional partner may actively resist changes which demand a greater share of responsibility for the family's well-

> *Expressing your warm feelings for another person is a highly assertive act.*

being. For the children, a whole new set of challenges is introduced, as they learn to deal with the requirements of increased self-reliance.

OUT OF THE MOUTHS OF BABES . . .

It has been said that "the last frontier of human rights is that of the rights of children." Despite the history of apparent dedication to individual rights in the United States, and even despite the hard-fought gains in rights for minorities, women, and others who have been denied and oppressed, we have made few changes in our basic notions that children are second-class citizens. The glorification of "youth" in popular media, dress styles, music, and literature has not carried over into a comparable respect for the rights of those who are very young.

Without debating the relative concerns of innocence and inexperience vs. age and wisdom, let us simply suggest that assertive children, like assertive adults, are likely to be healthier and happier, more honest, and less manipulative. Feeling better about themselves, these youngsters are headed toward more self-actualized adulthood.

We favor a conscious effort in families, schools, churches, and public agencies to foster assertiveness in young people. Let's create conditions which will tolerate — even support — their natural spontaneity, honesty and openness, rather than sacrificing it to parent anxiety and school authority.

Let us be clear — we do not advocate totally permissive child rearing. The real world places limits upon us all, and children need to learn that fact early if they are to develop adequate life s-u-r-v-i-v-a-l skills. However, we consider it vital that families, schools, and other child-rearing social systems view children as human beings worthy of respect, honor their basic human rights, value their honest self-expression, and teach them the skills to act accordingly.

Assertive skills are valuable for children in dealing with their peers, teachers, siblings and parents. When Mike Emmons led assertiveness groups at a local elementary school (grades 1-6), the youngsters got enthusiastically involved, and volunteered a few situations from their daily experience:

> *What do you do if someone pushes in front of you in lunch line?*
> *My sister borrows my things without asking. What should I say?*
> *When it's Joe's turn to be "out" in handball, he won't leave.*
> *What do you do if someone teases you or calls you names?*
> *The woman I babysit for forgot to pay me. I told my Mom, but she said I should call her. I am too embarrassed.*

The children easily understood the meaning of assertiveness. They practiced the skills, and especially enjoyed being videotaped in the process. Even the children's feedback to each other was specific and helpful. Children can learn the basics of assertiveness and apply them to situations in their own lives.

Parents often have difficulty discriminating between assertion and aggression when disciplining or dealing firmly with their youngsters. The definition of assertiveness applies to parent-child relationships! Although each situation is unique, the key to defining assertiveness in family interactions is *mutual respect.* Children, like parents, are individual human beings. They deserve fair treatment, and non-aggressive discipline.

Most of the principles and procedures advocated elsewhere in this book apply to the development of assertiveness in children, so we won't present any specialized material here. Interested readers may wish to consult the books *Liking Myself,* and *The Mouse, the Monster, and Me,* written directly for younger children by psychologist Pat Palmer. How about your kids? Have you taught them appropriate assertive skills? Can they handle themselves with their peers, with neighborhood bullies, with pushy salespeople, with privacy questions online, with adults who might take advantage of them? Can they openly express affection and appreciation to friends and relatives? You can teach them these and other assertive skills, using the procedures you've learned in this book. You'll learn a lot about them – and yourself — in the process!

THEY DO GROW UP, DON'T THEY?

Independence from our parents may be the single most important life issue we all face, certainly it is the core around which growing up revolves. Some rebelliousness is normal and healthy for teenagers, and facilitates their developing independence. Families with dominant parents and inhibited teenagers may find the teens' necessary steps toward independent adulthood are delayed.

Unresolved ties with parents — unfinished work from the teen years — sometimes restricts independence in the lives of adults of all ages. In our experience, an assertive approach by the "child" can clear the air, make the situation clear to the parent, and allow needed expression of feelings on both sides.

Such a confrontation is almost inevitably painful, and it is a considerable risk for both parent and child to open up old wounds. Despite this obstacle, we believe continued silence exacts much too high a price. Adults who avoid dealing with their parents or adult children as they would any other adult with whom they feel a special closeness can suffer unmeasured guilt, self-denial, inhibition, repressed anger, and often depression.

New York psychologists Janet Wolfe and Iris Fodor have done excellent work with the relationship of adult mothers and daughters, and their five steps toward a new assertive mother-daughter relationship are useful for anyone who is dealing with this issue:

. . . Recognize the life cycle issues each party is dealing with (eg. economic independence, menopause, retirement, etc.)

. . . Identify attitudes or beliefs which inhibit assertive communication (eg. "Don't talk back to your father.")

. . . Figure out the rights and goals of each party.

. . . Identify emotions (eg. anxiety, guilt) which interfere with pursuing goals.

. . . Try out new forms of relationship (eg. Adult-to-adult, rather than parent-to-child).

REGAINING BALANCE IN THE FAMILY SYSTEM

Let us sum up this discussion of assertiveness in the family this way:

❖ Assertive behavior enhances both individuals and relationships.

❖ Honest, open and nonhurtful assertive communication is desirable and highly valuable in families.

❖ Children as well as adults should learn to be assertive within the family — and beyond it.

The principles and procedures for defining and learning assertiveness, which are described in this book, are applicable to adults and to children (i.e., modeling, rehearsal, feedback, practice, reinforcement, mutual respect, and individual rights).

Change in family systems is more difficult, more time and energy consuming, and potentially more risky (families can and do break up) than is change in individual behavior. We encourage you to evaluate carefully, to proceed slowly, to involve everyone openly, to avoid coercion, to tolerate failure, and to remember that nobody and no approach is perfect! Notwithstanding these cautions, we also encourage you to work toward the development of an "assertive family." It can be a tremendously exciting and growth enhancing environment in which to live.

ASSERTIVENESS IN A SHRINKING WORLD

A final note before we leave this chapter on relationships. All of us live in networks which begin with ourselves as individuals, touch family and friends closest to us, and include neighbors, membership groups, community, region, nation, hemisphere, world (even the universe?). Events which happen in the next block, the next town, a nearby state, even across the world can have lasting effects upon our lives.

And we know about those events in moments: the Internet, CNN, shortwave radio, the local evening news, even the print media. The changes, and the speed with which they come at us, are mind-boggling.

People all over the globe are asserting their independence — declaring their rights of freedom and self-determination. As local autonomy, nationalism and independence are increasingly asserted world-wide, let's remember our own world citizenship in the process. The earth is small; we can't afford to be arrogant any more about political boundaries. Relationships with others begin at home, on the block, and down in town; but they must extend to our fellow human beings all over this tiny globe. At risk is our continued existence as a species.

14

Anger Is Not a
Four-Letter Word

When angry, count five;
when very angry, swear.
— MARK TWAIN

TWAIN WAS HALF RIGHT, at least. Counting to five — or fifty — may be a pretty healthy way to deal with angry feelings after all. (Just don't allow your hostility to escalate as you count!) Turns out that swearing, on the other hand, may not be such a good idea.

For more than thirty years, we've taught and written about ways to spontaneously and assertively express anger. Recent research, however, indicates that *expressing* anger — assertively or otherwise — may not always be the way to go. In this chapter, we'll take a look at the latest facts — and some myths — about anger, and suggest how it's possible to handle your anger and stay healthy.

SOMETIMES, YOU JUST CAN'T WIN!
Miles took his car to the local dealership for some routine maintenance work. The dealer's shop doesn't take appointments, operating instead on a first-come, first-served basis. Miles arrived at 8 A.M., and told the service manager he would pick the car up around 4:30 that afternoon.

Here's what happened when Miles came back for his car:

Miles: "Hi. I'm Miles Z., and I'm here to pick up my car."

Service Manager (looking through his worksheets): "I'm sorry, sir, we haven't gotten to your car yet."

Miles: "What? Why not? Man, that's really irritating! I made a service appointment, and I was here at 8 o'clock this morning. What happened?"

Service Manager: "Hey, you know how it is. This was just one of those days. We put your car in the back and got busy and just didn't get to it."

Miles: "Hell, that doesn't do *me* any good! It's damned inconvenient for me to get my car in and leave it all day."

Service Manager: "I know that, sir, and I apologize. I promise to get it done first thing in the morning if you want to bring it back."

At this point, Miles has a choice to make: persuade the service manager to have someone fix his car by working overtime; take his car elsewhere; return the next day for the repair work; demand a loan car; shout louder; threaten to contact the Better Business Bureau . . .

Miles so far has expressed his anger without being aggressive toward the service manager. He was rightfully mad, and told the manager so without downgrading him as a person. He might have responded aggressively, "You can take that repair job and shove it," or "You damn S.O.B.s better fix my car *right now!*" and stormed out. Either statement would likely inflame the service manager, further agitate Miles himself, and not accomplish much toward getting the work completed. Could he have handled it better?

NO EASY ANSWERS ABOUT ANGER

We keep looking for simple answers.

We elect public officials who offer glib solutions to the incredibly complex issues of the day, as if the good guys and the bad guys could still be identified by the color of their hats. We try to oversimplify relationships between apparent "causes" and their "effects." We want the answer to "Why do I behave that way?" to be simple. "Because you were toilet trained too early." "Because your family was dysfunctional." "Because you're a middle child." We search for effortless equations to "explain" the mysteries of the complex human organism.

Anger is one of those things that's an easy target for such simplistic psychology. It is variously seen as "sinful" (and therefore to be avoided at all costs), "freeing" (and therefore to be expressed at all costs), and all of the options in between.

Although there is considerable controversy among professionals who work in the anger field, there are some important points of *agreement:* (1) Anger is a natural, normal, human emotion; (2) Anger is not a style of behavior (although it is common to confuse emotions and behavior); (3) Chronic anger can be a major health hazard; (4) We can — and should — learn to defuse most anger even before it begins; (5) When we must express anger, we should learn to do so effectively: toward resolution, not revenge.

These five points give us a solid foundation from which to examine some of the popular *myths* about anger.

ANGER MYTH #1: ANGER IS A BEHAVIOR

Let's begin our exploration of anger myths by clearing up one widespread misconception. Anger is not a *behavior,* it's a *feeling.* The confusion of angry feelings with aggressive behavior has made it difficult for many people to effectively handle this natural, universal, and useful human emotion.

Some folks say, "I never get angry." We don't believe it! Everyone gets angry — that is, everyone experiences the *feeling* of anger. However, some people have learned to control themselves so that they do not openly *show* anger; they choose not to express their anger. By minimizing anger in your life, and developing nondestructive ways to deal with the anger you do experience, you can make aggressive actions unnecessary.

ANGER MYTH #2: YOU SHOULD BE AFRAID OF YOUR BURIED ANGER!

Anger remains one of the most difficult emotions for many people to express. Assertive behavior training groups often lose members when expression of anger becomes the topic. Many have "buried" their anger for years, and are terrified of the potential consequences should they ever "let it out." They assume that any anger brought into the open will be hurtful to others. "I'd sooner suffer in silence than to hurt anyone," is the common, unfortunate plea.

Yet much pain in human relationships results from anger which is unresolved. Both persons suffer. The angry one silently fumes. The other person continues to behave in ways that are upsetting, and wonders why the relationship is deteriorating.

But the answer to dealing with long-buried anger may not be what you think. It does not lie in pillow-pounding, or shouting at an empty chair, but rather in finding ways to resolve — within yourself or outside — the problem that caused the anger in the first place.

ANGER MYTH #3: THE HUMAN STEAM KETTLE

For many years, psychologists and the general public believed the old Freudian myth that human emotions are like a "steam kettle." In this view, strong emotions build up inside us somewhere, and if we don't vent them somehow, they'll eventually explode. The popular expression of this was, "You need to get the feelings out!" The idea was that by *expressing* the anger, the feelings would be released and prevent health problems associated with "building up inside."

Contemporary research has shown the concept to be false. We now know it doesn't work that way. What does happen is that we *remember* annoying events, and our feelings of anger can be experienced again when those memories are tapped. There are important differences between a "steam kettle" of simmering emotion and a "memory bank" of stored experiences. A steam kettle, for example, needs only release of its pressure build-up; memories can be satisfied only by solving the problem somehow.

ANGER MYTH #4: VENTING IS GOOD FOR YOUR HEALTH

One of the most persistent points of disagreement among anger researchers has to do with the value of "venting" angry feelings. Many theorists favor the use of pillows, foam bats, and other "harmless" devices, or shouting at an empty chair, as tools for physical "release" of angry feelings. Others point to research which demonstrates that teaching people such means of expression *strengthens* the angry feelings, and teaches them to vent their feelings aggressively even at "unsafe" times (such as when the other person is present and a violent fight may ensue).

What's more, contrary to the popular myth, angry feelings are not "released" through aggressive acts. The result of pillow pounding, shouting obscenities — and, yes, football or boxing — is that one simply learns ways to handle anger aggressively.

The best and most current evidence clearly supports the view that *venting angry feelings is not psychologically healthy.*

Physical expressions of hostility *do nothing to solve the problem.* Banging the table, stomping the floor, crying, striking at the air, hitting a pillow — all are devices for temporary expression of strong feelings without aggression toward another person. However, they are not effective methods for dealing with your anger.

A subset of the venting myth comes from the important work of Dr. Carol Tavris, a social psychologist whose studies of anger as a social phenomenon are widely recognized as accurate and authoritative. Among the myths Dr. Tavris has identified:

Myth: Aggression is instinctive catharsis for anger. *Reality:* Aggression is an acquired cathartic habit.

Myth: Talking out anger gets rid of it. *Reality:* Overt expression can focus or even increase anger.

Myth: Tantrums are healthy expressions of anger. *Reality:* Tantrums, if rewarded, teach the child a method of controlling others. "Emotions are subject to the laws of behavior."

Dr. Tavris' highly acclaimed, Anger: The Misunderstood Emotion, is one of only two books on the subject that we can recommend without reservation. (We'll talk more about the second book in a page or two.)

ANGER MYTH #5: ANGER NEEDS TO BE EXPRESSED

In early editions of this book, over twenty years ago, we encouraged readers and our clients to try *physical* approaches when learning how to express strong emotions: pounding a pillow; shouting "NO!" or "I'm really ANGRY!"; tug-o-war with a towel.

Later research — to our dismay — showed that when people *learned* those techniques, they *used* them — in therapy or out — often destructively. If no pillow was at hand, they might pound the nearest person!

So we shifted our emphasis to "non-destructive" *verbal* expression of anger, teaching folks to speak up without inhibition at injustices — real or perceived.

But research on human emotions doesn't stand still. Now, we must once again respond to new evidence about anger. This time it's medical science which has thrown us a curve, and questioned some aspects of the "spontaneous expression" approach. The latest research comes from long-term studies of the effects of hostility on the heart.

ANGER MYTH #6: TELL OTHER PEOPLE,
BUT NOT THE PERSON YOU'RE ANGRY WITH

All too often, people express anger, frustration, or disappointment with another person by indirect, hurtful methods. If you want to change the behavior of the other person, these approaches are rarely successful.

Newlyweds Martha and John are a "classic" case. In the first few months of their marriage, Martha discovered at least a dozen of John's habits that she disliked. Unfortunately for both, she was unable — or unwilling — to find the courage to confront John openly with her concerns. Martha instead chose the "safe" way to express her dissatisfaction with John's behavior; she confided in her mother. Worse yet, not content with almost daily telephone

Relief from anger comes only by some resolution to the problem.

conversations with mother about John's shortcomings, she also used family get-togethers as occasions to berate John before the rest of the family.

This "see-how-bad-he-is" style — telling a third person (or persons) about your dislikes of another — has disastrous effects on a relationship. John feels hurt, embarrassed, and hostile about Martha's attacks. He's angry that she didn't choose the privacy of their own relationship to tell him directly. He's not motivated to change his habits. Instead, he responds to her aggressive approach with bitterness and a resolve to strike back — by intensifying the very behaviors she would have him change.

Had Martha asserted herself directly by telling John her feelings, she would have created a good foundation for a cooperative effort to change both John's behavior and her ineffective response to it.

If John had responded assertively early in the process, he might have prevented the escalation of Martha's attacks and avoided the bitterness and growing resentment. Instead, his determination to get revenge is sure to drive a further wedge into the relationship. John and Martha seem sure bets for marital therapy and/or the divorce court.

"WHY DO I GET SO ANGRY?"

You'd probably like to know more about your own angry reactions to people and events. Here are some elements to look for as you answer that question for yourself:

Your genes. The data is not all in yet — indeed, the data may never *all* be in — but the best evidence in psychological science now suggests that about half of our personalities is genetically hard-wired. That is, we're born with certain behavioral predispositions. To some extent not yet fully understood, our "anger thermostats" are among those in-born traits. This factor is one you can't do much about, of course, but don't get discouraged. The others are largely subject to your control.

Your environment. Let's set the scene for anger. Where and when do you get angry? Consider the temperature, pollution, weather. Were you caught in a traffic jam? Pushed around in a crowd? Waiting in a slow line? Do you live under political oppression? Economic hardship? Are you a member of a minority which is often treated unfairly? (Lots of folks have good reasons to *start the day* angry.)

Your health. Do you have any significant disabilities? Are you fatigued much of the time? Under tension? Do you eat a balanced nutritious diet? Have you had a physical exam recently enough to be sure that your internal chemistry is right? Any of those factors can make it more likely that you will get angry if the right situation comes along.

Your attitudes and expectations. Do you believe the world should treat you fairly? Is it important to you to have people recognize your accomplishments? Do you have a strong sense of justice? Are there certain "right" ways things should be done? Rules everybody should live by? Such attitudes, beliefs, and expectations — while very human — can set you up to get angry at the way the real world treats you and others.

Your job. Do you work with unreasonable people? Are you happy in your personal and intimate relationships? Is your work satisfying and rewarding? If you are out of a job, you may be close to anger all the time.

Spend some time thinking — and writing in your log — about the anger in your life. Look for patterns. Pay special attention to what triggers your anger and how you express it. Discovering the patterns and targets of your anger are key to understanding — and dealing with — your emotional response.

FACTS, THEORIES AND MYTHS ABOUT ANGER

On the following page is a chart which summarizes some current notions about anger, classified under three headings: *facts* — findings which are clearly demonstrated by careful research, or are self-evident; *theories* — ideas for which there is some solid evidence, but which lack clear validation, and sometimes lead us astray; and *myths* — ideas which, despite their acceptance, have been proved wrong, or which appear on the surface to be accurate but contain false assumptions. The chart represents a summary of what is known about anger, according to our analysis of the most recent careful studies.

ANGER MAY BE HAZARDOUS TO YOUR HEALTH

For over three decades we've watched with interest and learned much from the work of California cardiologists Meyer Friedman and Ray Rosenman on "Type A" behavior. Their early results suggested that hard-driving, ambitious, angry men — so-called "Type A" personalities — were significantly more heart-attack prone than their "Type B" brethren — those whose style is more laid-back, relaxed, easy-going. The concept was widely accepted, and tens of thousands of men tried to convert themselves from Type A to Type B. Later research, however, failed to confirm the Type A hypothesis, and it lost respectability for a time.

Recently, Type A is back, qualified by an important new finding from the heart patient studies. Seems it's not Type A behavior as such that causes heart problems, but hostility (as measured by such well-established psychological tests at the *Minnesota Multiphasic Personality Inventory*), which is the key factor in heart disease. Psychiatrist Redford Williams and his colleagues at Duke University have identified a "hostility syndrome" — a collection of attitudinal and behavioral characteristics — which predicts heart disease with astonishing accuracy.

The Duke hostility research, with a large number of patients, shows three major factors in toxic anger: *cynical thoughts, angry feelings,* and *aggressive behavior.* Incidentally, most of the heart

ANGER: FACTS, THEORIES, AND MYTHS

FACTS	THEORIES	MYTHS
Anger is a feeling, with physiological components, not a mode of behavior.	Shy people, depressed people, and suicides are expressing anger at themselves.	Venting (by yelling, pounding pillows, hitting with foam bats) "releases" anger and therefore "deals with" it.
Anger is universal among human beings.	Anger should always be contained until it can be expressed in a calm, rational manner.	Anger should always be expressed spontaneously/ immediately.
What really matters is resolving the issue. Thus, the method of anger expression is important.	Men in our culture are able to express anger more easily than women.	Women are less angry than men.
Venting of anger – "catharsis" – is of value only insofar as it sets the stage for resolution.	Women are generally inhibited in anger expression by their social conditioning in our culture.	Some people never get angry.
Aggressive expression leads to further aggressive expression, not resolution.		Anger is always a "secondary" emotion, with another "real" feeling behind it.
Anger is not a "steam kettle" phenomenon: It does not build up and finally explode.		TV violence, active sports and/or competitive work "releases" anger.
Most anger is directed toward those close to us, not strangers.		Aggressive behavior is instinctive in humans.
Chronic hostility increases the risk of heart attack.		Anger is always a destructive, sinful, undesirable emotion.
Defusing anger is the healthiest way to deal with it.		Verbal expression of anger is always desirable.

Everyone gets angry.

Some people do not openly show anger.

research has studied men, but limited data on women show a similar pattern.

Williams's work was presented to popular audiences in 1994 in a national bestselling book, *Anger Kills,* co-authored with his wife, Virginia Williams. (This is the other book we recommend on anger.) Although the facts are not quite as dramatic as the title would suggest, the picture is not pretty. Chronic anger can be deadly.

Colorado State University psychology professor Charles Cole is another researcher who has found a definite health risk for people who are chronically angry. Cole studied 50 heart patients, and learned that the large blood vessels constricted — causing reduced blood flow, increased blood pressure, and risk of a heart attack — for some patients when they merely *discussed* subjects they were angry about. For the chronically angry — those who are angry most of the time — says Cole, the constriction of blood flow is also chronic, and heart attacks may be much more likely.

So what does this new information mean to our use of assertive methods to express anger? Are we simply to "take a deep breath" and forget the feelings? Is it really healthiest not to even *talk* about our anger?

Stay tuned.

IS IT EVER OK TO EXPRESS ANGER?

"I'm confused. On the one hand you're saying, 'It's not healthy to express anger.' On the other, you say, 'You need to resolve your anger; don't let it become chronic.' Which is it? Do we show anger or not?"

We warned you that there are no simple answers. Human emotions are incredibly complex, and there aren't any "one size fits all" solutions. There are some guidelines, however, and the rest of this chapter is devoted to helping you sort out the complexities.

To begin our examination of healthy ways to respond to angry feelings, Williams and Williams offer a "Hostility Roadmap":

❖ "Is the matter worth my continued attention?"

❖ "Am I justified?"

❖ "Do I have an effective response?"

They're suggesting that, when you begin to feel angry, you take a moment to consider just how big a deal this *really* is, and how right you *really* are. (In chapter 19 we've provided a detailed guide to choosing when to take assertive action.) Then, if you decide that your angry feelings *must* be expressed, do so assertively, without hurting someone else (physically or emotionally) in the process.

Honest and spontaneous expression *aimed at resolving the disagreement* can help to prevent inappropriate and destructive anger later, and may even achieve your goals at the outset. When you do choose to express your anger, one of the most constructive steps you can take is to *accept responsibility for your own feelings.* Keep in mind that *you* feel the anger, and that doesn't make the other person "stupid," "an S.O.B.," or the cause of your feeling.

The central objective of effective anger expression should be to achieve some *resolution of the problem* that caused the anger. "Getting the feelings out" — even in appropriately assertive ways — only sets the stage. Working out the conflict with the other person, or within yourself, is the all-important step that makes the difference. That doesn't mean pounding a pillow until you are exhausted; it means working out some *resolution* of the issue yourself — through relaxation, forgiveness, attitude change, negotiation, confrontation, or psychotherapy.

If you take action which doesn't help you to cope or to resolve the problem, your anger may actually increase, *whether you've expressed it or not.* So, focus your energy on problem-solving actions. Work to resolve the issue through assertive negotiation of solutions with the person with whom you have been angry. If direct resolution is not possible, find satisfaction within yourself (perhaps with the aid of a therapist or trusted friend). In either event, don't stop by saying, "I'm mad as hell!" Follow through with " . . . and here's what I think we can do about it . . ."

Keep your anger in perspective. Don't take it too lightly, or too seriously. Learn what triggers it, teach yourself to "lighten up" in the face of situations that usually set you off, and develop effective ways to deal with it when it comes.

"So What Can I Do About My Anger?"

We'd like to offer you a simple, three-step method for dealing with anger in your life. We'd like to, but we can't. Anger is a complex phenomenon, and handling it is complex as well. Fortunately, however, there are some really helpful procedures which are of proven value. As it happens, they fall naturally within three general guidelines: 1) minimize anger in your life; 2) cope before you get angry; and 3) respond assertively when you get angry.

Minimize Anger in Your Life

Our first ten steps are borrowed from the Williams' recommendations in Anger Kills:

1. *Improve your relationships* with others through community service, tolerance, forgiveness, even caring for a pet.

2. *Adopt positive attitudes* toward life through humor, religion, acting as if today is your last day.

3. *Avoid overstimulation* from chemicals, work stress, noise, traffic.

4. *Listen to others.* Practice trusting others.

5. *Have a confidant.* Make a friend, and talk regularly, even before you feel stress building.

6. *Laugh at yourself.* You really are pretty funny, you know. (It goes with being human.)

7. *Meditate.* Calm yourself. Get in touch with your inner being.

8. *Increase your empathy.* Consider the possibility that the other person may be having a really bad day.

9. *Be tolerant.* Can you accept the infinite variety of human beings?

10. *Forgive.* Let go of your need to blame somebody for everything that goes wrong in life.

To the Williams' ten, we add two of our own to this "anger-in-your-life" section:

11. *Work toward resolution* of problems with others in your life, not "victory."

12. *Keep your life clear!* Deal with issues when they arise, when you feel the feelings — not after hours/days/weeks of stewing about it. When you can't deal with it immediately, arrange a specific time when you can and will!

COPE BEFORE YOU GET ANGRY

Anger is a natural, healthy, non-evil human emotion and, despite our best efforts to minimize its influence in our lives, all of us will experience it from time to time, whether we express it or not. So, in addition to the steps above, you'll want to be prepared before anger comes:

13. *Remember that you are responsible for your own feelings.* You can choose your emotional responses by the way you look at situations. As psychologists Gary McKay and Don Dinkmeyer put it, *How You Feel Is up to You.*

14. *Remember that anger and aggression are not the same thing!* Anger is a feeling. Aggression is a style of behavior. Anger can be expressed assertively — aggression is not the only alternative.

15. *Get to know yourself.* Recognize the attitudes, environments, events, and behaviors which trigger your anger. As one wise person suggested, "Find your own buttons, so you'll know when they're pushed!"

16. *Take some time to examine the role anger is playing in your life.* Make notes in your log about what sets you up to get angry, and what you'd like to do about it.

17. *Reason with yourself.* (Another good idea from the "Williams collection.") Recognize that your response will not change the other person. You can only change yourself.

18. *Deflect your cynical thoughts.* Williams suggests thought stopping, distraction, meditation.

19. *Don't "set yourself up" to get angry!* If your temperature rises when you must wait in a slow line (at the bank, in traffic), find alternate ways to accomplish those tasks (bank by mail, find another route to work, use the time for problem solving).

20. *Learn to relax.* Develop the skill of relaxing yourself, and learn to apply it when your anger is triggered. You may wish to take this a step further by "desensitizing" yourself to certain anger-invoking situations (see chapter 10 for more on desensitization).

21. *Develop several coping strategies* for handling your anger when it comes, including relaxation, physical exertion, "stress inoculation" statements, working out resolution within yourself, and other procedures, such as those suggested by the Williams' (items 1-10 above) and those we've noted in the box at the end of this chapter.

22. *Save your anger for when it's important.* Focus instead on maintaining good relationships with others.

23. *Develop and practice assertive ways to express your anger,* so these methods will be available to you when you need them. Follow the principles you've learned in this book: be spontaneous when you can; don't allow resentment to build; state your anger directly; avoid sarcasm and innuendo; use honest, expressive language; let your posture, facial expression, gestures, voice tone convey your feelings; avoid namecalling, putdowns, physical attacks, one-upmanship, hostility; work toward resolution.

Now you've developed a healthy foundation for dealing with angry feelings. Go on to the following section and get ready to handle your anger when it comes.

RESPOND ASSERTIVELY WHEN YOU GET ANGRY

24. Take a few moments to *consider if this situation is really worth your time and energy,* and the possible consequences of expressing yourself. (Remember the Williams' "road map" described earlier in this chapter.)

25. *Take a few more moments* to decide if this situation is one you wish to work out with the other person, or one you will resolve within yourself.

26. *Apply the coping strategies* you developed in step 21 above, and those listed at the end of the chapter.

If you decide to take action:

27. *Make some verbal expression of concern* (assertively). The sidebar on the next page may give you some helpful ideas.

28. *"Schedule" time for working things out.* If you are able to do so spontaneously, fine; if not, arrange a time (with the other person or with yourself) to deal with the issue later.

29. *State your feelings directly.* Use the assertive style you have learned in this book (see #23 above), with appropriate nonverbal cues (if you are genuinely angry, a smile is inappropriate!).

30. *Accept responsibility for your feelings.* You got angry at what happened; the other person didn't "make" you angry.

31. *Stick to specifics and to the present situation.* Avoid generalizing. Don't dig up the entire history of the relationship!

32. *Work toward resolution of the problem.* Ultimately you'll only resolve your anger when you've done everything possible to resolve its cause.

Here are a few verbal expressions others have found useful for expressing anger:

"I'm very angry."

"I'm getting really mad."

"I strongly disagree with you."

"I get damn mad when you say that."

"I'm very disturbed by this whole thing."

"Stop bothering me."

"That's not fair."

"Don't do that."

"That really pisses me off."

"You have no right to do that."

"I really don't like that."

"I'm mad as hell, and I'm not going to take this anymore!"

WHEN SOMEONE ELSE IS ANGRY WITH YOU

Okay, now you know how to deal with your own anger. But one of the most important needs expressed by assertiveness trainees is for ways to deal with the anger of *others*. What can you do when someone is furious and directing her full hostility at you?

Try these steps:

❖ Allow the angry person to vent the strong feelings.

❖ Respond only with acceptance at first ("I can see that you're really upset about this.")

❖ Take a deep breath, and try to stay as calm as possible.

❖ Offer to discuss a solution later — giving the person time to cool off ("I think we both need some time to think about this. I'd like to talk with you about it . . . in an hour / . . . tomorrow / . . . next week.")

❖ Take another deep breath.

❖ Arrange a specific time to pursue the matter.

❖ Keep in mind that no immediate solution is likely.

❖ Follow the conflict resolution strategies described below, when you meet to follow up.

CONSTRUCTIVE RESOLUTION OF ANGER AND CONFLICT

How can we improve the process of resolving angry conflict between people or groups? Most of the principles are parallel to the methods of assertiveness training presented throughout this book, and many overlap our discussion earlier in this chapter of ways to deal with anger.

Conflict is more easily resolved when both parties want to work things out, of course. Here is a set of proven guidelines for those who are willing to try:

❖ Act honestly and directly toward one another.

❖ Face the problem openly, rather than avoiding or hiding from it.

❖ Avoid personal attacks; stick to the issues.

❖ Emphasize points of agreement as a foundation for discussion of points of argument.

❖ Employ a "rephrasing" style of communication, to be sure you understand each other. ("Let me see if I understand you correctly. Do you mean...?")

❖ Accept responsibility for your own feelings ("I am angry!" not "You made me mad!").

❖ Avoid a "win-lose" position. The attitude that "I am going to win, and you are going to lose" will more likely result in *both* losing. If you stay flexible, both can win — at least in part.

❖ Gain the same information about the situation. Because perceptions so often differ, it helps to make everything explicit.

❖ Develop goals which are basically compatible. If we both want to preserve the relationship more than to win, we have a better chance!

❖ Clarify the actual needs of both parties in the situation. I probably don't need to win. I do need to gain some specific outcome (behavior change by you, more money), and to retain my self-respect.

❖ Seek solutions rather than deciding who is to blame.

❖ Agree upon some means of negotiation or exchange. I probably would agree to give on some points if you would give on some!

❖ Negotiate toward a mutually acceptable compromise, or simply agree to disagree.

Almost everybody has trouble with anger, and there are no easy answers for dealing with this complex emotion. There are some things that help, however. Remember these four key guidelines:

❖ *Minimize the anger in your life.*

❖ *Cope before you get angry.*

❖ *Be assertive when it's important to express your anger.*

❖ *Work to resolve conflict whenever it occurs.*

15

Must We Put Up with Put-downs?

He that respects himself is safe from others;
he wears a coat of mail that none can pierce.
— HENRY WADSWORTH LONGFELLOW

REMEMBER THOSE TIMES IN LIFE when you felt belittled by somebody? The feeling may have resulted from a look, expression or shrug. Or someone's words may have provoked a feeling of worthlessness.

You feel perplexed. Instead of feeling up, you start to doubt yourself and feel down. Put-downs provoke a cloud of darkness or confusion and may stand out in your mind for years.

You say, "Of course there are a lot of put-downs. That's because there is so much to criticize!" Perhaps. People do scowl at looks, dress, lifestyle, mannerisms, work performance, speech. It's easy to come up with ways to let others know they are not OK.

Most of us add to the problem of put-downs from others by putting ourselves down as well. If you were traveling to a distant location and remembered en route that you'd forgotten to bring something you'll need when you get there, what would you do? If you're like most of us, you'll likely let go with some expletive or caustic comment about your "stupidity." Only the most sensitive and self-disciplined among us have presence of mind enough to take a deep breath, forgive ourselves for being human, and look for a way to solve the problem and move on — in short, to "deal with it."

In this chapter, we'll explore some of the most common put-down behaviors and what to do about them; specifically: the *direct verbal* put-down; the *indirect verbal* put-down; the *nonverbal* put-down; and the *self* put-down.

THE DIRECT VERBAL PUT-DOWN: "YOU FOOL!"

This type of behavior is obvious: another person is verbally "dissing" you. Imagine, for example, that you're leaving an elevator and accidentally bump into someone. That person responds immediately in a hostile manner: "Watch yourself, damn it! You fool! You could have hurt me!" The intent of such an in-your-face over-reaction is obvious. Should you respond? How?

Here are the steps we have found effective in dealing with a direct verbal put-down:

❖ allow the person to vent feelings, and to slow down;

❖ acknowledge the other person's feelings;

❖ when you are wrong, admit it, even in the face of insult;

❖ assert yourself about the way he or she is reacting;

❖ make a short comment to bring the encounter to an end.

These steps will help resolve a put-down encounter where the intent is out in the open.

In the elevator incident you could first let the person vent until the angry feelings slow down. As the outburst subsides, you could take a deep breath, then say, "I apologize for bumping into you. It was accidental. Obviously you are upset, but I don't like to be called names or yelled at. I can get your point without that." Try to stay calm, and avoid a confrontational tone, facial expression, posture, or gestures.

INDIRECT VERBAL PUT-DOWNS: "NICE WORK, FOR A WOMAN."

How about this one, from your boss? "You did a nice job on that project you turned in yesterday. All the grammatical errors gave it a folksy quality." Or, what if your spouse says, "I love the way you look when you wear that outfit; old clothes become you." Do you do a double-take? Are you confused? What are the real meanings behind statements of this kind?

Such indirect verbal put-downs are *indirect aggression*. In their book, *The Assertive Woman*, Stanlee Phelps and Nancy Austin describe indirect aggressive behavior by observing: ". . . in order to achieve her goal, she may use trickery, seduction, or manipulation." They note that others react with confusion, frustration, and a feeling of being manipulated. Indirect aggressive behavior comes out as a concealed attack; Phelps and Austin label the person who behaves in this manner a "mad dog in a lamb's suit."

Handle an indirect verbal put-down first by asking for more information. In either of the situations given above, you might reply with, "What are you saying?" or "What do you mean?" Such a response tends to help clarify the person's true intent (you may have misunderstood).

Your second response will depend upon the other person's answer. Part of your goal in the situation, however, is to teach the person a new way of behaving toward you. If the boss indicates on the second exchange that, "Oh, I think you did a good job," you might still want to say, "Well, thank you, but I was a little confused. If you're really concerned about my errors in grammar, I hope you'll say so directly. I couldn't really tell if you thought the project was good or bad." You're trying to teach the boss to be straightforward with you. (Hint: Think of comics character "Sally Forth.")

In marriage relationships, some good-natured teasing can be fun. Too often, however, underlying hostilities come out in the guise of teasing. Your spouse may have been kidding you all along, but there are more straightforward and less destructive ways to do so.

What if your spouse isn't kidding? Imagine that her next response is even more aggressive. We suggest that you remain assertive, following the steps given above for direct verbal put-downs. Be prepared to go further with your assertion if the response to your inquiry is another put-down.

On the other hand, when you ask for clarification, you may get some valuable information about your behavior. Remember that a major goal of assertive behavior is to level the playing field, to permit *both* people to express themselves openly and honestly. It's difficult for most of us to give direct feedback about another person's upsetting behavior, so we often camouflage our comments by an indirect put-down style. Digging further may help your future relationship with that person.

Nonverbal Put-downs: Dirty Looks and Obscene Gestures

"Sticks and stones may break my bones, but words will never hurt me" is a taunt children long have used to rebuff name-callers. Unfortunately, no reply has yet been invented for our adversaries who put us down *without* words. What's the best way to respond to an obscene gesture or a dirty look? How should pouting and silly grins or smirks be dealt with when the person uses no words to help you verify the meaning?

Nonverbal put-downs are much harder to deal with because there are no words in the first place, and the person may not even be consciously aware of the put-down. And you can't really be sure you accurately read the nonverbal message.

If another person aims an obviously *aggressive* nonverbal put-down toward you, try to get the person to use words instead of gestures. You might say assertively, "I'm not sure what you're saying. Could you translate that look (gesture) into words for me? I have trouble knowing what you're feeling unless you tell me directly." Again, remember to avoid confrontational non-verbal behavior yourself. Be prepared for a verbal put-down at this point and respond according to the suggestions given above.

The *nonassertive* nonverbal put-down is the least direct of all. If you're making a request of someone who begins to stare off into space or grin, the intent is not so obvious as if the person aggressively shakes a fist in your face. There is a good chance that the person who responds with an indirect nonverbal put-down is doing so automatically, out of habit. We all have mannerisms which take the place of words.

Imagine you are about to pay for a purchase when the cashier looks at you, rolls her eyes, and sighs in an exasperated way. You may wish to write it off as nothing personal, or merely assume the cashier is having a bad day. If you're bothered by the incident, however, why not deal with it directly? Ask him to explain: "I didn't understand your expression," or, "I'm not sure what you mean by that," or, "Did I do something you didn't like?" This places the nonverbal response out in the open, to clear the air.

If you have done something that bothers somebody else, you deserve to know. Your next response will depend on what happens then, but we think it is a good idea to point out to others it's difficult to interpret their nonverbal messages.

SELF-PUT-DOWNS: "I'M SUCH A JERK"

Outer conflict, such as that described above, is only half of the picture. Inner conflict can also result in put-downs. The offender in this case is *you*. Put-downs are generated by conflicts, external or internal. The solution is the same — be assertive.

You can behave nonassertively or aggressively *within* yourself as well as toward others. Be careful about how you deal with yourself. Try not to take flight (nonassertively) and neglect or escape your inner put-down behavior. Don't be too caustic and condemning (aggressively) with your inner thoughts and feelings either. Take the middle ground: deal with yourself assertively. Be honest, open, straightforward with yourself. Try to figure out the source of your inner conflict. Use the situation as an opportunity to get to know yourself better.

SUMMARY

No one likes the conflict generated by put-downs. By risking an open and straightforward clarification, with the other person or yourself, the discord can be resolved.

It does take some constraint to avoid feeling hurt and withdrawing or lashing out. The rewards of honest communication are usually worth the effort.

Don't condemn or run away from put-downs, your own or another's.

The upset caused by put-downs can be resolved if you will "put your assertive foot forward." Be persistent in clarifying the situation with yourself or the other person.

Do you have to put up with put-downs? No! You can learn ways to respond assertively, clear the air, express your feelings, resolve the conflict (real or imagined), and gain new information about yourself and your relationships.

16

Assertiveness, Intimacy, and Sexuality

Live all you can;
it's a mistake not to.
— WILLIAM JAMES

SSERTIVENESS, INTIMACY AND SEXUALITY may seem to be strange bedfellows (pun fully intended), but the subjects actually have a lot to do with each other. Assertiveness has many applications in the realm of intimate relationships. This chapter offers a brief introduction — we cannot give them all the space they deserve here — but you can use this material together with the procedures you've learned in earlier chapters to improve your assertiveness in the intimate and sexual relationships in your life.

INTIMACY AND SEX ARE NOT THE SAME THING

Many people use the words *intimacy* and *sex* interchangeably. They define sexual expression and intimate expression in the same breath, as if they were equal.

They're not.

Intimacy includes much, much more than sex. Think of it this way: if you put a tiny pinch of cinnamon into a bowl filled with a host of other ingredients, it adds a zing of flavor to the final outcome. Sex is like that touch of cinnamon. It adds zing, but it is far from the whole recipe.

As a result of our interest in assertive, equal relationships, we've devoted intensive study to the factors which contribute to healthy intimate partnerships. In our book, *Accepting Each Other*, we described six vital dimensions of intimacy. Sex didn't make the first team. It's important, of course, but it's a second-string player.

Don't misunderstand. We don't underestimate the significance of the sexual relationship. It's just not the all-important factor lots of folks make it out to be. Even though the media constantly bombard us with sexual images, when anybody bothers to ask couples how important sex is to their overall happiness most rank it below such intimacy variables as communication, understanding, and commitment. You can guess why. True intimate sexual expression is a result more than it is a cause of overall healthy intimacy. While the prevailing myth would have us believe that sex is the best indicator of a happy couple, the reality is that happiness is dependent upon the total relationship. Sex is but a small part.

If not sex, then what is intimacy?

Here's our definition:

> *Intimacy is a quality of relationship, between two people who care deeply about each other, which is characterized by mutual* **attraction**, *open and honest* **communication, commitment** *to continuation of the partnership,* **enjoyment** *of their life together, a sense of* **purpose** *for this relationship, and mutual* **trust** *which honors and respects each other.*

Genuine intimacy is a complex blend of those six major dimensions, which also (not by accident) fit the acronym ACCEPT. This model of intimacy embodies the idea of *acceptance* of yourself, of each other, and of your relationship. Acceptance is truly the heart of intimacy.

It's worth noting too, that all intimate partnerships are *interdependent systems*, in which the two individuals, the six dimensions of their relationship, and their environment are constantly interacting.

Intimacy is a vital thread which weaves through virtually every aspect of a love relationship. When it's healthy, it helps increase a couple's happiness, satisfaction, and fulfillment, improving their communication, attitudes, love for each other — and sex life.

As you think about assertiveness in intimate relationships, keep sexuality in perspective — it is just one part of total intimacy.

Is That All There Is?

The importance of sexuality varies with the couple involved, of course, and without a sexual relationship, a key way to express love is lost. If sex is primary, however, the relationship may be shallow —and fragile.

In very intimate relationships, as between lovers, it is often assumed that each partner knows the feelings of the other. Such assumptions may lead to the marriage counselor's office with complaints such as, "I never know how he feels," "She never tells me she loves me," "We just don't communicate any more." Frequently it's necessary to rebuild a communication pattern which allows each partner to express caring feelings openly. The expression of caring won't solve all the ills of an ailing marriage, but it can "shore up the foundation" by helping each partner remember what was good about the relationship in the first place!

Psychologist Arnold Lazarus of Rutgers University has identified two-dozen "myths" which create major problems in many relationships. In his book, *Marital Myths Revisited,* Lazarus suggests that the myth, "True lovers automatically know each other's thoughts and feelings," is particularly destructive of intimate relationships. Lazarus's advice? Don't take it for granted! Don't assume! Communicate!

But it doesn't help to beat your partner over the head with "self-disclosure." The most basic fact about intimacy is that, by its very nature, it is shared with another person, but taking the idea of "sharing" to extremes can get you in trouble. Telling your partner "everything" *telling* under the guise of "total honesty" is an exercise in emotional self-indulgence that may result in greater distance between you, rather than increasing closeness. Don't sacrifice your relationship on the altar of *unreserved* self-expression. And if you do, don't bother to call it "assertive"!

YOU'RE NOT ALONE!

In 1975, the World Health Organization recognized the complexity in a formal definition of sexual well-being:

> Sexual health is the integration of the somatic, emotional, intellectual, and social aspects of sexual being, in ways that are positively enriching and that enhance personality, communication, and love.

As if your own personal sexuality were not intricate enough, society — government and the prevailing mores *customs* — gets into the act too. (Duh! Doesn't it always?) Intimate relationships weave together the two individuals, their partnership, and the society in a highly complex fabric of attitudes, emotions, physiology, mores, customs, values — even politics and economics.

Nobody ever said it would be easy.

Amazing, isn't it? You'd think that the complexity of sexual expression combined with the complexity of intimate communication would be enough to deter any sane person from engaging in either, let alone both!

But it doesn't, of course.

ARE "MARS AND VENUS" REAL?   *AMEN*

No. It sounds cute, but we're not from different planets. And it's certainly misleading (at the least) to suggest that all women are one way and all men another!

In the late twentieth and early twenty-first centuries, we have moved from a time of heavy emphasis on the physical aspects of sex to a focus on the relationship aspects. Instead of exploring for new erogenous zones, we are talking about true intimacy, about <u>communication</u>, <u>devotion</u> and <u>commitment</u>. Some see all this as a swing back to the "good old days." It seems more accurate to consider the entire process an evolution, of which the so-called "sexual revolution" — at least the increased openness of expression about sexual topics — was a key part. The new emphasis on commitment incorporates the <u>gains</u> made through increased sexual expression. There is no return to the old times, or forgetting about recent discoveries.

Whatever we call them, the changes of recent decades dug deeply at the closely-held attitudes, beliefs, stereotypes, and behaviors which inhibited complete sexual expression. Although traditional values were questioned, they were not abandoned. Now we are <u>moving ahead with newfound abilities, openness, awareness, and equality.</u>

The "Female and Male Sexual Attitudes and Behaviors" chart on the following page summarizes society's former and current sexual expectations for men and women.

And the process of change continues.

Both sexes are still overcoming blocks to healthy sexuality. Couples today are able to build their sexual relationships on the foundation of new knowledge and techniques, greater freedom of sexual expression, and a new equality between the sexes.

Where are we headed? The <u>cornerstones</u> of the new sexuality are <u>communication</u> and <u>commitment</u>. The new vocabulary includes <u>words like</u> assertiveness, adult-to-adult, negotiation, devotion, faithfulness, fidelity, and intimacy. We are entering a new era of togetherness . . . and taking with us the new knowledge about the physical aspects of sex.

ASSERTIVE SEXUALITY

In earlier chapters, we discussed self-expression as a need of all humans. Sexual expression is a special application of the principles of assertiveness we have presented throughout this book. Anxiety, skills, attitudes, obstacles . . . all are elements of sexual communication, along with the components of verbal and

FEMALE AND MALE
SEXUAL ATTITUDES AND BEHAVIORS

FEMALES

FORMER EXPECTATION	CURRENT EXPECTATION
Passivity	Equality
Misguided compassion	No-nonsense compassion
Silence and suffering	Outspoken enjoyment
Giving In	Initiation
Doing your duty	Active participation
Hunting	Straightforwardness
Manipulation	Honesty
Shyness, embarrassment	Confidence, playfulness
Fragility, weakness	Strength, helpfulness

MALES

FORMER EXPECTATION	CURRENT EXPECTATION
Silence	Expression
Lack of emotion	Openness, flow
Insulation	Involvement
Strength	Vulnerability
Control	Mutuality
Machismo	Gentleness
Inflexibility	Patience
Exploitation	Equality
Score keeping	Responsiveness

non-verbal behavior described in chapter 6. What you have already learned about assertiveness is a good foundation for your assertive sexual communication.

One element which does seem to come up more frequently in sexual relationships than elsewhere is indirect aggression — so-called "passive-aggressive behavior." This is the style which is designed to make the other person feel guilty or bad, or to put responsibility on the other, or to manipulate the other into doing something. A variety of inventive methods are employed: false flattery, coyness, pouting, seeking sympathy, whining, crying, finding fault, playing "hard to get," even lying.

The "Sexual Communication Types" chart (pages 162-163) depicts four styles for expressing feelings about sexual interaction. For each style, five subcategories help narrow down our meaning: trait descriptions, inner thoughts, outer expressions, affect, body language.

There are several important considerations to keep in mind about the four types of sexual communication:

First, none of us is purely one type or another. Each person may lean heavily one way, but we all exhibit all four behaviors at times. Come on now, admit it, even you! You have been known to pout a little or come on too strong or ineptly fumble around, haven't you? And, of course, there are times when you are quite confident, direct and assured. We would all like to be purely assertive, but no one is perfect!

Second, the goal in sexual communication is to have the capability and choice to respond as you like. Many of us respond by default, lacking the skills, attitudes, or behaviors necessary to be fully aware and in control of our sexual expressions. Those who keep working at it, however, do begin to find their relationships more satisfying and fulfilling.

Third, the motivation for some behavior is beyond our awareness. We fool ourselves. Of course, we think that we always understand why we react in certain ways, but depth psychology indicates differently. Feelings that are unresolved seem to appear in unexpected forms of behavior.

SEXUAL COMMUNICATION TYPES

BEHAVIOR	TRAIT DESCRIPTIONS	INNER THOUGHTS
Nonassertive	Hesitant, shy	"She's being way too rough with me during sex."
		"He hurt my feelings when he said I wasn't much into sex tonight."
Indirectly Aggressive	Devious, manipulative, sneaky	(Upset that he's been told no) "I'll get her goat... insinuate she's been having an affair."
		"Ugh, sex tonight! I'll pretend to be terribly ill."
Aggressive	Demanding, pushy, insistent	"That's a stupid way to caress me!"
		"Why doesn't he ever want to have intercourse a different way? He is so straight!"
Assertive	Honest, open, straight-forward	"Our foreplay has been really short recently."
		"She hasn't seemed to be as responsive to me lately."

OUTER EXPRESSIONS	AFFECT	BODY LANGUAGE
"Did you think you were a little bit rough tonight?"	Irritated	Obscure
"I'm sorry, I wasn't very good tonight."		Hidden
"Did you read in the paper that people who aren't interested in much sex with their spouses are usually having affairs?"	Angry	Incongruent
Yawns, looks distressed, sighs, frequently rubs stomach and makes a face.		Subversive
"You're so clumsy tonight!"	Hostile	Abrasive
"Are you crazy? Everyone is into this!"		Confrontive
"It seems to me that foreplay hasn't been very long lately. I enjoy it and would like it to last longer."	Bright	Forthright
"I have been feeling that you aren't as responsive during intercourse lately."		Direct

Fourth, all sexual communication is two-way, of mutual concern. This brings us back to devotion and commitment. Keep in mind your purpose. It isn't manipulation, or deceit, or always pleasing the other person, or being right. It is working things out together, realizing that you both play an equal part in your sexual communication.

Fifth, body language and spoken language are both vital in sexual expression. The chart hints at the key components. Keep in mind that sexual assertiveness is much more than the words you use. Perhaps here, more so than in other types of situations, body language is vital!

SEX IS A SOCIAL ACTIVITY

New knowledge and greater sexual expressiveness brings increased responsibility. Safe sex, teen pregnancy, HIV-AIDS, abortion, promiscuity, prostitution, assault — the social issues around sexual behavior are almost overwhelming. Sex is not just something that happens between two people in the privacy of their relationship.

A book on assertiveness is not the place for an extended discussion of these issues, but in advocating an assertive lifestyle, including assertiveness in sexual matters, we must address a few of our major concerns, especially when they are topics in the news virtually every day. We don't presume to offer solutions to these major social problems, but a few comments are in order:

❖ *Sex education for children belongs in the home, AND in the schools, AND in the media.* There is no legitimate evidence that education our young people about their bodies and about the sexual and reproductive processes increases the likelihood that they will engage in sexual activity prematurely. There is abundant evidence that lack of adequate sex education leads to unwanted teen pregnancies and sexually transmitted diseases.

❖ *Young people must learn to speak to others openly about sex.* The vast majority of sexual assaults are committed by acquaintances, friends and — unspeakably — family members. Each of us must learn to respect and protect our bodies, and to say no directly and assertively to unwanted sexual advances. That learning should begin at an early age, preferably at home.

❖ *Each person has a fundamental human right to self-determination.* It is a basic tenet of assertiveness, as discussed throughout this book, that each of us has the right to be and to express ourselves, and to feel good (not powerless or guilty) about doing so, as long as we do not hurt others in the process.

❖ *Knowledge of safe sex practice is critically important to every adult and young adult.* The statement on pages 168-169 provides guidelines on this topic.

SAMPLE SEXUAL SITUATIONS CALLING FOR ASSERTIVENESS
Here are a few examples to help you understand each type of sexual communication better, including a "typical" response for each type.

BEACH BLANKET ROULETTE
Richard was really excited. He had been pursuing Susan for weeks now, and they finally had agreed to a picnic at his favorite — virtually private — spot on the beach. It was a beautifully warm afternoon, and Susan had worn a particularly sexy bikini. As the day waned into evening and their ardor warmed, Richard asked, "How about making love here on the beach?"
Susan wasn't sure. She liked Richard, but . . . She said:

a) "Are you sure you're man enough, Mr. Hotpants?"

b) "That sounds like fun, but I really need to be home in 20 minutes."

c) "Uhh, sure, if you want to . . ."

d) "I'd like that. I have a condom and spermicide in my purse if you didn't bring them."

BEDROOM BOREDOM

During the past six months your partner has become less sexually attentive. You've been having intercourse less often, and your partner is not as enthusiastic or caring when you do. You've tried hard to provide motivation, but to no avail. Your frustration leads you to try this:

a) You decide to be more patient. It crosses your mind that you are not sexy enough. You try being more attentive to your partner's every need.

b) You tell your partner that you went to the doctor and were told that your hormone levels are low. You hint that more intercourse would be helpful.

c) You lash out irrationally. Your feelings of upset have built to a boiling point. This evening's dull sexual encounter was the "last straw." Your partner retaliates. The verbal explosion lasts for hours. You are still seething and spend the night on the couch and the next week sulking.

d) You tell your partner that your patience is exhausted, and that there must be a change in your sexual relationship. Your style is firm, but not confrontational. You suggest alternatives: a new self-help book you've read about; a weekend workshop conducted by a sex therapist; an appointment for relationship counseling. Your partner is reluctant, replying, "You go; it's your problem." You persist, acknowledging that some of the difficulty lies with you, pointing out that it affects you both. You repeat your desire that you both work on the problem.

ALCOHOL AMOUR

Your partner routinely drinks too much before you have intercourse. You feel that the drinking interferes with the quality of sex, and that it's time to take action:

a) You hesitantly ask if there is "any chance that you might be drinking a little too much before intercourse?" Your partner is offended and responds defensively, "It's just normal social drinking."

b) You begin talking about the "evils of alcohol" to others in front of your partner at social gatherings. At home you "misplace" the alcohol; when you do serve drinks, you "accidentally" drop your partner's drink.

c) In the middle of intercourse you yell out, "You're a drunken slob!", dramatically pull away, and storm off to sleep on the couch.

d) Talking directly to your partner at a relatively calm and private moment, you express your concern that the drinking before intercourse is interfering with the quality of sex for you. You give more details in a straightforward way, emphasizing that your relationship together is very important to you.

Some Basic Skill Areas of Assertive Sexuality

There is a basic landscape of sexual communication, key situations that repeatedly arise in relationships. Here are several, along with a few suggested "words of wisdom" which you may find useful.

❖ *Saying No.* Because of the sensitive nature of sexual communication, it doesn't hurt to use a little empathy and understanding in the process of saying no.

> *"I am not trying to hurt your feelings, but no, I don't want to do that."*

> *"I love you, but I am really too tired tonight. How about tomorrow night?"*

(Situations which call for more than a simple "no" are discussed in the next section.)

❖ *Saying Yes.* We all like a little enthusiasm, especially when we propose something amorous!

> *"Sure. I'll go for that!"*

> *"That sounds neat. Yes."*

> *"Yes, let's have intercourse tonight."*

IMPACT STATEMENT ON SAFE SEX

The management, many authors, and editorial advisors of Impact Publishers, Inc. – predominantly professionals in the human services – recognize safe and healthy approaches to sexual expression as one of the principal health and social issues of our time. We offer the following statement for your serious consideration:

❖ Sexual expression is a basic, normal, positive, intensely personal and highly satisfying human activity. Although sexual practices are often publicly regulated by social mores, religious values, and law, individuals and couples decide privately whether or not to follow such regulations.

❖ Responsible sexual practice requires good information, including knowledge of the fundamentals of human sexuality, responsible family planning, contraceptive choices, and protection against sexually transmitted diseases.

❖ Sexually transmitted diseases, such as Acquired Immune Deficiency Syndrome (AIDS), various forms of Herpes, Hepatitis B, and the several Venereal Diseases, are serious and widespread public health problems, both in the United States and throughout the populated world.

❖ "Safe sex" — minimizing the risks of sexually transmitted diseases — includes at minimum the following:

an absolutely certain, long-term monogamous relationship, or *ALL of the following:*

– regular, periodic physical examinations;

– conscientious unfailing use of condoms (preferably with spermicides) during intercourse;

– awareness and avoidance of common risk factors in STD's (e.g., intravenous drug use, high-risk populations);

– honest and open discussion of sexual habits and preferences with potential partners;

– infrequent changing of partners.

❖ Each individual — married or single — has the right to freedom of choice in sexual expression, so long as the practice involves consenting adults and consciously avoids physical or psychological harm to any person.

❖ No one is obligated to have a sexual relationship with another person — including a marriage partner — unless he or she wishes to do so.

❖ The following AIDS facts are reproduced from the brochure, *Understanding AIDS: A Message from the Surgeon General*, released in 1988 by C. Everett Koop, M.D., then Surgeon General of the United States:

—*The AIDS virus may live in the human body for years before actual symptoms appear.*

—*Who you are has nothing to do with whether you are in danger of being infected with the AIDS virus. What matters is what you do.*

—*There are two main ways you can get AIDS. First, you can become infected by having sex — oral, anal, or vaginal — with someone who is infected with the AIDS virus. Second, you can be infected by sharing drug needles and syringes with an infected person.*

—*Your chances of coming into contact with the virus increase with the number of sex partners you have.*

—*You won't get AIDS through everyday contact...a mosquito bite...saliva, sweat, tears, urine, or a bowel movement...a kiss...clothes, a telephone, or from a toilet seat.*

—*A person can be infected with the AIDS virus without showing any symptoms at all.*

— *Condoms are the best preventative measure against AIDS besides not having sex and practicing safe behavior.*

RISKY BEHAVIOR

- *Sharing drug needles and syringes.*
- *Anal sex, with or without a condom.*
- *Vaginal or oral sex with someone who shoots drugs or engages in anal sex.*
- *Sex with someone you don't know well (a pickup or prostitute) or with someone you know has several sex partners.*
- *Unprotected sex (without a condom) with an infected person.*

SAFE BEHAVIOR

- *Not having sex.*
- *Sex with one mutually faithful, uninfected partner.*
- *Not shooting drugs.*

— *If you know someone well enough to have sex, then you should be able to talk about AIDS. If someone is unwilling to talk, you shouldn't have sex.*

❖ *Being Playful/Breaking New Ground.* Why should sex be dull and boring, or the same all the time? Why not take risks, explore with each other, try something new? We need a freer, more imaginative and playful approach to sexuality.

> *"Honey, I've been reading this new book and I'd sure like to try position number 85 tonight."*

> *"How about a massage with almond oil? We'll even light some incense!"*

> *"Let's only kiss and fondle tonight. No intercourse."*

❖ *Listening.* The above situations involve speaking out. The other side, listening, is a lost art — especially when it comes to close, personal, intimate relationships. Take time to *hear* what your partner is saying.

Marital therapists often assign homework to help couples improve their listening skills. For example, try repeating back what your partner says and getting confirmation that you have heard the message correctly before you reply. Then have your partner do the same thing: fully, accurately listen to you before replying. It certainly can help you to feel heard and valued!

❖ *Negotiating/Compromising.* These are skills that are helpful in all aspects of marriage or relationship. Learning to give and take, to let it be known what you desire, to take turns, are all necessary in assertive sexuality.

WHEN NO IS NOT ENOUGH

Sexual coercion and assault of women is a major social problem in our society. Estimates and research findings vary widely, but it appears that at least a quarter of all women over age 18 have experienced some form of unwanted sexual activity. Most such unfortunate events involve friends, relatives, or dates. Only a small percentage are actually committed by strangers. Too many women cannot say no and make it stick — and too many men are behaving like spoiled children who won't take no for an answer.

Since women are most often the victims of unwanted sexual advances, the vast majority of programs for dealing with the problem have been directed to them. Until societal attitudes change significantly, and men begin to accept responsibility for treating women with respect, such efforts will continue to center on arming women with self-protection techniques. Assertiveness training has been used with great effectiveness in this area.

Here are a few suggestions for developing your own assertive approach to preventing unwanted sexual advances:

❖ Prepare yourself for building your assertiveness skills.

❖ Talk about it openly with dates and co-workers.

❖ Be clear from the onset — set limits.

❖ Don't create expectations.

❖ Don't send double messages.

❖ Say no firmly when limits are exceeded.

❖ Demand that your partner, (date, co-worker) take responsibility.

❖ Leave yourself an out (don't get trapped).

❖ Raise your voice if you are ignored.

❖ Report violations to appropriate authorities.

If you are a woman reading this, we urge you to take steps to improve your assertiveness in responding to such situations. Practice your "saying no" skills in a variety of circumstances, particularly those which would involve you in situations you prefer to avoid. For our male readers, we offer a strong invitation to reconsider your own attitudes about women, about sexuality, about the rights of each person to self-determination, and about respect for each other. If you tolerate or encourage other men to "prove themselves" sexually, you are contributing to the problem even if you yourself do not engage in coercive behaviors. If you assume that dinner and/or a show, or a few dates, or even a promise of a future relationship "earns" you the right to a sexual relationship against the will of your partner, you are still caught up in the "macho mode," and we urge you to think about how you might act if you really accepted a woman as your equal in the relationship, and if you were to treat her with the respect that equality demands.

ASSERTIVENESS AND EQUALITY IN INTIMATE RELATIONSHIPS

We have often pointed out in this book that genuine assertiveness is a means for establishing equality in a relationship, not simply for expressing your own needs. Nowhere does that fact have more direct application than in the realm of intimate partnerships. In a relationship characterized by equality, love, and honest assertive expression, the intimate dimension can grow to immense mutual satisfaction. Without those qualities, a fulfilling intimate relationship is unlikely.

Assertiveness Works at Work, Too

*Worthy are the labors
which give us a sign
other than age to show
that we have lived.*
— LEON BATISTA ALBERTI (1503)

TO BE ASSERTIVE ON THE JOB can be particularly difficult. Fear of reprisals from supervisors or co-workers, even fear of losing the job itself, are formidable obstacles for many.

Yet there are countless ways to express yourself assertively at work. In this chapter, we'll explore several, including some examples to help you see how assertiveness can work for you.

Let's start with a few general ideas about how you can practice assertion on the job:

❖ Put off procrastination.

❖ Improve your decision-making skills.

❖ Negotiate more effectively.

❖ Deal with angry customers, bosses, coworkers, other difficult people assertively.

❖ Learn to say no so you'll not lose yourself. (Most organizations will take all you'll give, and expect more. If co-workers know you can say no, they won't be reluctant to ask you because they know they'll not be "imposing.")

❖ Be persistent: plant a seed and nurture it.

❖ Be patient. Assertiveness is not necessarily in a hurry.

❖ Speak up about health and safety issues in the workplace. You may risk your job, but that beats risking a limb or a life.

❖ Improve your time management by taking more control of yourself and your schedule.

❖ Be assertive about goal-setting on the job. Realistic goals, assertively pursued, are more likely achieved. There are, of course, those who would make it difficult for you to express yourself openly on the job (no news there!). Such obstacles may come in the form of manipulation (ignore these), unreasonable requests (you can simply point out the unreasonableness), and reasonable requests (which you may not be able to handle, and will need to say so).

Sometimes performance anxiety becomes a problem in the workplace. Overcoming anxiety was the original reason for assertiveness training, and is still an important application of the process. Making public presentations, for example, is reportedly the number one fear of Americans. That fear can be "desensitized" by taking gradual steps toward expressing yourself to others, beginning with one or two friendly folks, and working up to a larger group of co-workers and/or strangers.

Problem solving, negotiation, and conflict resolution on the job can be aided through creating an atmosphere which allows — even encourages — constructive disagreement. As different ideas are expressed, it becomes possible to work out compromises that build in the strengths of everyone's contributions. Solutions that are the result of brainstorming by a number of people are often winners; creative juices are stimulated by letting all thoughts come out without censorship or critique.

We've arranged the balance of this chapter in its natural sequence, from the process of job and career search, through landing a job, working well with others, to being a supervisor. The chapter concludes with some questions about your priorities, and a potpourri of work situations for your own assertiveness practice. It may help to read all of the material, or you may prefer to turn directly to that aspect of job-related assertiveness which fits your specific interests and needs.

JOB SEARCH

When we graduated from college (back in "olden times"), jobs were plentiful for anyone with a degree. Things have changed a lot; jobs can be tough to get in many fields these days, with or without a college education. Widespread layoffs result as large corporations merge and slim down, or as smaller firms find it difficult or impossible to stay afloat amongst the giants. Competition among job hunters can be fierce.

Looking for a job can be a full time "job" in itself. Many people seem to expect to put out a few applications, make a few calls, have an interview or two, and land the job of their dreams. Unfortunately, that is a dream. Finding the work you want takes work — and assertiveness can be one of your most useful tools.

Richard Nelson Bolles, in his bestselling book *What Color Is Your Parachute?*, presents a comprehensive plan for "Job Seekers and Career Changers." His counsel is as good as you'll find anywhere, and applies the concepts of assertiveness with a broad brush. Bolles's innovative and practical ideas will help you learn about your own career desires and needs, locate opportunities, make contact with employers, handle interviews, and land the job you want.

Among Bolles' recommendations for an assertive approach to careers:

❖ Plan your career and your job search with a clear goal in mind: decide what you want to do, where you want to do it, and for whom.

❖ Seek out activities you enjoy: you'll go after them with more enthusiasm, do them better, and be satisfied longer.

❖ Claim the highest level of skill you legitimately can: you are more likely to find a job and the job can be more uniquely tailored to you.

❖ Find and meet the employer you want to work for: show the person who has the power to hire you just how you can help fill the needs of that organization.

INTERVIEWING

Even if you have followed Bolles' advice and created your own job, you'll likely go through some traditional interviews along the way.

Now at last an employer has offered you an opportunity to meet and discuss an opening! You've worked hard for this chance to tell what you can do, and you are really looking forward to it. You are pretty anxious, too. After all, getting the job depends largely upon how well you present yourself in that short meeting.

Assertiveness can help. We suggest you take it as it comes:

BEFORE THE INTERVIEW . . .

Follow the principles we've described in this book to develop your own assertive skills

Prepare yourself to deal with anxiety by practicing cognitive restructuring and relaxation (chapters 9 and 10).

Write down and memorize three or four key strengths you want to be sure the interviewer remembers about you; be sure to relate them specifically to the job in question.

Practice interviewing with a friend or counselor. If you can, use a video camera and recorder to capture a sample of your own style. Watch the tape, and let that feedback help you become even more effective.

AT THE INTERVIEW . . .

Approach the interviewer with a friendly, but not-*too*-well-rehearsed style.

Remember that most employers would rather hire someone with a strong desire to work and to contribute to the organization than a "star" who may try to outshine the current staff.

Try to relax, enjoy yourself, and get acquainted!

Let the interviewer know you've done your homework, prepared for the interview, and learned something about the company.

Ask good questions about the working environment, staff morale, advancement, employer expectations.

Avoid asking obvious questions you should have answered for yourself by some advance preparation (company product line, details about retirement and health benefits . . .).

Leave the interviewer with a sample of your work, or some other device which will cause him or her to remember you and your talents.

AFTER THE INTERVIEW . . .

Drop a note to the interviewer, expressing your appreciation for the meeting, calling attention to any important facts about you, and mentioning details which may have been missed in the interview.

Spend some time assessing and critiquing your own performance, so you'll be ready to do even better next time.

Continue to contact other employers and to arrange other interviews until you land the job you want!

After you accept the job, dedicate yourself to doing it well, but don't cut off the contacts you've established with other employers. You never know . . .

CAN THE "NEW KID ON THE BLOCK" BE ASSERTIVE?

When you do get that new job, it is important to start out by *listening* a lot. You'll need to find out as much as possible about the rules of the workplace, the attitudes and opinions of your supervisors and colleagues, the safety factors of the job, the expectations of your role and how it fits into the larger scheme of things, and much more.

But listening alone probably will not be enough to give you all the information you'll need. As you begin to learn your way around a new place of employment, it will be important to ask questions as well. And that's where assertiveness comes in once again.

Remember to maintain *balance*. You want to seem interested in the job, to show the boss and others that you are conscientious. At the same time, you don't want to be a constant nag, demanding more and more information — much of which may not even be relevant to your own work.

We suggest the following guidelines:

- *Do your homework.* Don't expect your boss or co-workers to fill the gaps in your preparation for the job (unless you are clearly in a training program).

- *Ask your supervisor* and co-workers the questions to which you must have answers in order to do the job.

- *Don't be too quick to ask,* since you may be told when the subject comes up in turn.

- *Make notes of other items* that occur to you, and ask them when the subject comes up.

- *Ask your boss about asking questions.* Does she/he prefer that you ask immediately, or in a regular conference, or when . . . ?

- *When you do ask questions, be assertive:* don't beat around the bush, don't start out defensively ("This may be a dumb question . . . "), try to focus your question on the specifics, use good eye contact, voice, timing, etc.

- *Avoid suggesting changes until you are well acquainted* with the operation.

- *Avoid the temptation to describe "how we did it at Acme Widget"* (or wherever you worked before) unless you're asked. Better to let it be your own idea — or let it go altogether.

ON-THE-JOB-RELATIONSHIPS

Getting along with others at work is essentially a process of making a place for yourself in the work group. At home, the family has little choice but to accept you. In school, although acceptance of your peers can be a tough burden, *you're* the one without choice: you *have* to be there.

The job, for most of us, does offer some choices. Unlike family or school ties, one *can* quit, although the price for doing so may be high. Getting along becomes a matter of deciding to make a place for yourself. And that means developing a relationship of mutual respect with your co-workers. (To have some fun with this topic, check out *The Dilbert Principle*.)

Here are some ideas which may help:

Stay honest; avoid game playing.

Count to ten before you sound off in anger (refer to chapter 14).

Listen to what the other person has to say — even if you disagree.

Ask yourself, "How would I feel in this person's shoes?"

Express your opinions, but remember they are opinions, not gospel.

Consider: Is it more important to be a "star," or to get the job done?

Be assertive when it matters.

Accept responsibility for your mistakes — and credit for your successes.

A couple of practice situations for you to think about:

- *A co-worker has been taking company supplies* home for personal use. She knows you are aware of this, and expects you to say nothing.

- *The woman at the next desk loves to chew gum* — loudly. You find the noise annoying and distracting.

- *A senior colleague has made repeated sexual comments* and suggestions, and frequently finds opportunities to touch you inappropriately.

DEALING WITH SUPERVISORS

Some bosses act as though they would have been happier in an earlier era, when all employees were virtual slaves. For the most part, however, the workplace has become quite civilized — even humanized. Supervisors still oversee, but they generally follow modern law and custom — and their own good sense — in treating their workers with respect.

Nevertheless, there are inevitable situations in which it is necessary, as an employee, to express an idea, opinion, or objection firmly, in the face of opposition from the boss.

Don't get caught in the trap of coming down on yourself every time you are criticized on the job. You may be wrong, but the way to deal with the situation is to correct the problem, not to kick yourself. Help your boss to make criticism *specific*, so you can make the adjustments needed to improve.

Assertive efforts to clarify the boss's expectations and criticisms will help clear the air, and will enable you to become more effective. If instead you act as a "victim" — mumbling to yourself or backbiting — you'll make no progress, and likely make a powerful enemy along the way.

Try to identify *patterns* in your boss's critiques. If you think you discover one, ask assertively if that *is* what the boss wants ("You'd rather have all the supporting data presented *with* my recommendations, wouldn't you?"). If you clear up any possible misunderstanding in this direct way, you'll save time — and similar criticism — in the future.

Timing may be the most important component of your on-the-job assertiveness — especially with the boss. If you confront a supervisor in front of others, or when the boss is very preoccupied with another problem, you aren't likely to gain a favorable audience. Instead, plan — and schedule if necessary — your feedback to the boss so that you can be alone and relatively uninterrupted.

Here are a few other examples of situations with supervisors for practice:

- *You have an innovative suggestion* for simplifying a routine procedure.

- *Your boss is making unreasonable demands* on your time, without offering additional compensation.

- *You are being unfairly criticized* for the quality of your work.

- *You know more about the job than your boss does,* yet she wants you to do it her way.

- *Your boss is asking you to do jobs* that you believe are his responsibility.

- *Your boss expects you to prepare "phony" expense accounts.*

- *You've been asked – at 4:45 – to stay this evening* and prepare a report for tomorrow's Board meeting. You have plans for the evening.

SUPERVISING ASSERTIVELY

Now you've done it! You've been so effective with your on-the-job assertion (along with some pretty good work!) that you've been promoted. Now *you're* the boss. New responsibilities, new opportunities, . . . new headaches!

How do the principles of assertiveness apply in the supervisory role? Can you get the job done, treat your staff with respect, and exercise appropriate authority — all at once?

There are many theories of management, and hundreds of good ideas about how to supervise others. While this is not the place for a comprehensive survey, the following guidelines blend our concept of assertiveness with some of the best:

- *Build your assertive managerial style* on the foundation of good on-the-job relationships described earlier in this chapter: honesty, responsibility, cooperation, teamwork, mutual respect.

- *Listen — and pay attention —* to what your people have to say.

- *Roll up your own sleeves* and work with your staff.

- *Walk around —* and find out first-hand what is needed.

- *Remember that we're all equal* on the human-to-human level.

- *Make your instructions clear and direct.*

- *Accept the responsibilities of leadership,* including decision-making.

- *Criticize fairly,* focusing on the performance — not the person.

- *Praise often,* focusing on the performance — not the person.

- *Consider:* a manager must both lead the staff and provide necessary support.

- *Include the following resources in your supervision "tool kit":* team building skills; clear communication of your expectations; skills in employee motivation; encouragement of assertiveness in your staff.

Here are a few supervisory situations for practice — and to help you keep things in perspective:

- *One of your employees has made a thoughtful proposal* for a new work procedure. You recognize the idea as one the General Manager would probably veto because of its start-up costs.

- *A supervisor of your rank from another department* comes into your area and wants to borrow some equipment. Company policy prohibits such transfers.

* *You are confronted by a young trainee* who refuses to follow your directions.

* *An employee under your supervision* is not working up to your standards. You wish to improve his performance.

* *Performance reviews are due next week.* You must critique a long-time colleague whose work is weak in several areas.

* *As a new crew chief* at an assembly plant, you are responsible for the work of several men old enough to be your father. At least one of the men believes his ways are right, and refuses to accept your authority.

* *A long-time employee in your department* has been coming to work late nearly every day this week, with no explanation.

* *You recognize that one of your workers is an alcoholic,* but she won't admit it or seek treatment.

KEEPING YOUR PRIORITIES STRAIGHT

Work can be really seductive. If you enjoy what you do, and if you are good at it, you'll probably be advancing in salary and responsibility frequently. As a result, you'll feel motivated to take on even more, and the cycle will go on.

That sort of involvement with your work can play havoc with your personal life — if you let it get out of hand. More and more, you'll take work home, stay late at the job, go in weekends, take business trips. You could wind up with little time left for yourself or your family.

Can you be assertive with yourself? Can you elect to pass up career advancement opportunities in favor of more time for home and family? What are your priorities? It's easy to *say,* "My family comes first." It's harder to act accordingly.

Others won't settle for less than "having it all." Career, family, community, self — all are juggled like oranges, at least for a while. The stresses of the real world seldom allow us to maintain that precarious balance for long.

Being assertive with yourself means clarifying your personal priorities, recognizing you cannot do everything — at least not all the time — making appropriate choices, and saying "no" when you've reached your limits. Keep your own goals in mind (refer to chapter 8 and your log as you need to).

Test yourself with a few related situations. What's *really* important to you?

• *You've been offered an important promotion* with your present firm. Actually, you'd been thinking of leaving, but the outside job you want is not yet available.

• *More and more evenings and weekends are spent working* on job reports. Your family is beginning to complain that you have no time for them. You think you have an opportunity for a major promotion if you keep up the pace.

• *You want to continue your successful career,* but you know that your only step up in the company will require going back to school for additional course work in business — maybe an MBA. Such a step will require postponing plans to have children — which you and your husband want very much.

MORE ON-THE-JOB SITUATIONS FOR PRACTICE

Use the step-by-step process in chapter 12 as a guide to build your skills, and practice handling the following work-related situations:

• *Your boss suddenly turns cool toward you,* but offers no explanation. You want to ask what's going on.

• *Although you have been in your job longer than anyone* in your department, you are a part-time worker. Nevertheless, you are often called upon to train others or answer questions as if you were a supervisor. You are paid less, and have no real authority.

• *You've had several job interviews recently,* but keep finding yourself acting in a very passive way. The interviewers seem disappointed that you do not "sell" yourself.

• *A manager in another department* — very powerful in the company — has been making not-so-subtle sexual advances toward you.

• *After you've spent many hours on a special report,* your boss's supervisor is highly critical of your results.

• *You've been asked to handle a job* which is clearly outside your responsibility and beyond your competence. You think it may be a "test" of how well you know your own limits.

Even if you are not working regularly now, chances are you will be sooner or later. Give some thought to the issues raised in this chapter. Use your log to keep track of your own on-the-job assertiveness, and how you can improve it. You'll be more effective in your work, more highly respected by your peers and supervisors, and enjoy yourself more!

18

Dealing with Difficult People

Don't interrupt me
when I am interrupting!
— WINSTON CHURCHILL

Y OU KNOW THE TYPE:

❖ He leans on your desk, glares, and says loudly, "Just how long is it going to take me to get some help around here?"

❖ She comes over from next door whining: "Are you folks ever going to clean up your yard? You know, your place is the only one on the block that . . ."

❖ He calls your business and demands immediate service, an extra discount, and extended terms. ". . . And if you can't help me, I want to speak to the owner."

❖ She can't wait to corner you at the open house: "Did you hear about Fred and Betty?" she hisses. "Wilma told me that they . . ."

What is a "difficult person"? *Anyone who doesn't behave as expected.* We do, after all have some unwritten "rules" about appropriate behavior in our society. Be fair; wait your turn; say "please" and "thank you"; talk in conversational tones and volume . . . Difficult people ignore those mores, or act as if they are exempt — often while they expect you to live by the standards they're flaunting. They're usually loud, intrusive, impolite, thoughtless, selfish, and, well, *difficult!*

What do difficult people get out of being that way? One of our all-time favorite answers to that question was given by a workshop participant: "The biggest cookie." They also usually gain control, get their way, and get attention.

Why do we give these troublesome folks what they want? Well, for one thing, it's usually easier than hassling with them. Most of us don't have the skills, the time, the energy, or the inclination to try to put such people "in their place." Sometimes, they show up in a business context, where the policy may be that "the customer is always right."

(Incidentally, we don't happen to think that's an enlightened perspective. Nobody is always right. A more workable view is that "the customer is always the customer," and the business is advised to treat customers well, fairly, and promptly.)

Other times, it seems more trouble than it's worth to try to confront such people. After all, it's highly unlikely that you'll change them, and you may even get into trouble for taking them on. So, what to do?

Actually, there are a few approaches that can pay off. In this chapter, we'll consider some of the possibilities.

What Do You Think?

What are your thoughts when you're confronted by a "difficult" customer, neighbor, co-worker? What goes through your mind?

❖ *"Here goes that SOB again."*

❖ *"Uh, Oh, I'm in trouble now."*

❖ *"What does he mean?"*

❖ *"We've got to fix that problem."*

❖ *"Let me out of here!"*

❖ *"No problem — I can handle it."*

❖ *"Take a deep breath."*

❖ *"How embarrassing!"*

❖ *"That's the funniest thing I've heard today."*

Your thoughts set the scene for how you'll respond to a difficult situation. Consider your own first reactions — and re-read chapter 9 for ideas on developing more constructive thought patterns — as you take a look at the options for action outlined below.

How to Deal with Bozos

The following discussion offers a "smorgasbord" of action steps you can take when confronted by someone who's trying to push you around. Draw on those which seem to fit your style and life situation, and put together a response plan for your own "difficult people." You may never need to fear them again!

1. Change Your Cognitions (Attitudes, Thoughts . . .)
"It's all in how you look at it."

Preconceptions, attitudes, beliefs, prejudices — all kinds of preconditioned thoughts are influential in determining our responses to daily situations. Those ideas may be about the way life is in general, the way your life is, the way this particular person is . . .

For example, if you believe that life is fair, and that things work out for the best, and that people are basically good, you'll probably respond very differently than you would if you believed that life is not fair, things usually go wrong, and people are no damn good.

Stress Inoculation is one procedure for dealing with cognitive responses. It involves systematic development of self-statements which will help you change your thoughts related to specific situations and people. The following examples are grouped according to four stages of a difficult event. (Refer also to the discussion of this technique in chapter 9.)

> *Preparation*
> Nothing to worry about.
> I've handled tough situations.
> I'll play my own game.

Confrontation
    Stay calm and focussed.
    This guy is human too.
    I know my job.

Coping Response
    Relax, breathe deeply.
    Fear and anger are expected.
    I can control myself.

Reprise
    I got through it okay.
    The problem will be resolved.
    It's over; I can relax.

2. Deal with Your Anxiety
"Dentist's Chair Syndrome" or, "If you're going to get drilled anyway, you might as well lie back and enjoy it."

A hostile confrontation usually causes the adrenaline to pump — at least at first — and raises the anxiety response. There are several actions on the "anxiety track," including

❖ Run away

❖ Tense up and freeze in place

❖ Relax and breathe deeply

❖ Systematic desensitization (Preparation before an anxiety producing event by deconditioning.)

You'll recall that chapter 10 has helpful ideas for dealing with your anxiety before and during a difficult situation.

3. Take Direct Action
"Don't talk to me like that!"

Assertive and aggressive responses fall into this category of action options: standing up to the attacker, saying you will not put up with such abuse, asking why he is so upset, ordering him out of your office, asking who the hell he thinks he is, telling him to go to hell . . . Handling the situation this way involves facing the person directly, speaking up in a firm voice, using gestures and facial expression which appropriately convey your determination not to be pushed around, taking the risk of possible escalation . . .

"When you come at me that way, I'm not moved to do what you ask."

4. TRY SYNTONICS
"Tune in, turn on, talk back."

We discussed this approach, developed by Suzette Elgin, in chapter 8. It is described in detail in Dr. Elgin's books on the theme, "the gentle art of verbal self-defense." Syntonics procedures involve getting in tune with the attacker, acknowledging her point, indicating your empathy with her emotion — but not giving in. Techniques include:

❖ Matching sensory modes (sight, smell, hearing,...)

"Do you *see* what I mean?" "I *hear* you." "That doesn't suit my *taste.*"

❖ Ignoring the bait, while responding to the attack.

Attacker: *"If you really wanted to do a good job . . ."*

Response: (Ignoring bait) *"When did you start thinking I don't want to do a goodjob?"*

Our late friend, psychotherapist Andrew Salter, called this "playing your own game, not the other guy's." This process is a sort of "applied go with the flow" — letting the other set the pace and style, but not going along with his/her intent. Your action is firm, but not confrontive. Such behavior makes you definitely not "fun" to pick on. Your objective here is to take control — to play your own game.

5. CONSIDER LIFEMANSHIP
"What's that on your cheek?"

Stephen Potter's "lifemanship" systems, including "one-upmanship," offer ways to get your antagonist off-balance. Among other things, Potter suggests in his books getting the advantage *before* you are attacked:

❖ "Is something wrong?" (looking at spot on forehead), or staring without saying anything, and denying that anything appears "wrong."

❖ "That ball was out!" (tennis)

❖ "Of course I had a reservation, guaranteed on my VISA."

❖ "When I had lunch with the Lt. Governor last week, he suggested . . ."

6. FIND SOLUTIONS
"No fault insurance."

Your response is to ignore any emotional content of an attack, simply dealing with the substantive issues involved, and seeking solutions to the problem:

❖ "I can see we need to work out a solution to this situation."

❖ "There really is a problem here. What do you suggest we do to avoid similar circumstances in the future?"

❖ "Let's take a look at the data and see if we can come up with some answers."

7. WITHDRAW
"The engagement is off!"

This approach involves either saying something simple and direct, such as "I'll be glad to discuss this with you another time — when you're not so upset," or saying nothing at all, and simply leaving the scene.

Some situations are not worth the energy it would take to resolve them at the time. This is especially appropriate when the attacker is rational but totally unreasonable (but not if violent).

8. USE HUMOR
"...and the world laughs with you."

Humor can be appropriate on almost any occasion. This works best, of course, if you have a natural joking style, and are pretty good with one-liners, so you can disarm anger or attack with a funny line. It doesn't mean telling jokes which might be funny under other circumstances!

Ask yourself: "How would Dana Carvey handle this?" "How would Rosie O'Donnell handle this?" "How would Bill Cosby handle this?"

9. KNOW YOUR AUDIENCE
"Not in front of the children!"

"A time and a place for everything" applies here. You may wish to offer an opportunity to discuss the matter at length in private, but point out your unwillingness to pursue it in front of others, since both parties may find it awkward, and a rational solution may be less likely.

10. REQUEST CLARIFICATION
"Say what...?"

A simple, direct request for clarification — especially if it is repeated a couple of times — can de-escalate a situation and help put you in control.

❖ "I'm not sure I understand."

❖ "What exactly is it that you want?"

❖ "Would you explain that to me again?"

Again, your goal is to gain a measure of control — to prevent manipulation — to play *your* game.

11. CHANGE THE SCENE
"Build a level playing field."

Particular individuals — maybe even some in positions of power — may regularly, predictably cause you grief. Or perhaps specific re-occurring situations — such as a routine on your job — are likely to produce certain kinds of problems. Then you may need to work with others to establish some institutional or departmental support systems which "cut 'em off at the pass." Such systems might include:

❖ Behavioral ground rules for meetings.

❖ Standard procedures for how you'll serve people.

❖ Policies you apply uniformly.

❖ Collective/departmental action to get institutional change.

THE SITUATION IS SERIOUS, BUT NOT HOPELESS

Here is a summary of guidelines and procedures which can help when you're confronted with a particularly difficult person or situation:

❖ Your efforts ought to be directed at *solving a substantive problem,* not "taking care of" a difficult person. If you insist on one "winner," there probably won't be one. (And if there is, it may not be you!)

❖ *De-escalation* of loud voice and angry gestures is usually best accomplished by modeling: lower your own level of emotional behavior and you'll probably affect the other person's actions.

❖ *Your approach to these situations should be your own* as much as possible — a good fit with your natural style. All the ideas here are legitimate — but only some will work for you.

❖ *Preparation in advance* is a big help. Learn deep breathing and relaxation techniques, cognitive restructuring, assertive skills. A confrontation is not the time to start practicing!

❖ If you're going into a situation where it's likely you'll confront a difficult person, *set up some ground rules* in advance to cover typical problems (e.g. time limits for talkers in a group meeting).

❖ If there are particular individuals in your life who are predictable problems, you can *practice methods which are custom designed* for responding to them.

❖ *Get to know yourself* and your own triggers for emotional response. As someone said, "Get to know your own buttons, so you'll know when they're pushed!"

❖ So-called *"I-messages" really can help* — take responsibility for your own feelings without blaming the other person.

❖ *Acknowledging the other person's feelings while seeking a resolution* is usually helpful. ("I can see you're really upset about this.") But be especially careful not to patronize or come off sounding like a too-empathetic Rogerian counselor.

❖ It's often not possible to solve a situation on the spot. *Look for a temporary way out* so you can seek a solution in a calmer moment.

❖ Remember, *you do have some options* for action. Any of them can cause you more trouble with a difficult person if you become a manipulator, so apply them sensitively — but firmly — and with the main goal of getting on with your life.

Part V

Living an Assertive Life

Deciding When
to Be Assertive

Two roads converged in a wood, and I —
I took the one less traveled by,
And that has made all the difference.
— ROBERT FROST

THROUGHOUT THIS BOOK, we've emphasized that assertiveness is, first and last, a matter of personal *choice*. Don't "assert yourself" just because you can. Don't "assert yourself" every time life rankles you a bit. Don't go out of your way to look for opportunities to "assert yourself." When — as will happen from time to time — the natural course of things produces a situation in your life that could really be *improved* by speaking out, that's the time to put your assertive talents to work.

"So how do I know when action is called for?"

In this chapter we've outlined a "baker's dozen" questions to ask yourself when you're considering, "What do I do now?" Honestly consider each of these questions, and use the answers to help you decide when to be assertive . . . and when to let it go.

1. What really happened?

Are you sure you understand the situation clearly? Have you heard both sides?

2. How much does it matter to you?

How does this situation relate to your life goals? Will assertive action now achieve something important for you? Have your values been violated? Have you acted on similar situations in the past? Is someone's safety or well-being involved? A job? A promotion? Is an important principle at stake? Have you thought about your motivations for action in the situation? Would you be acting just to "be assertive"? Is this something you feel "should" be done, or will you and others actually benefit?

If your spouse leaves the top off the toothpaste, it may irritate you, but how important is it in the larger scheme of things? How about making a game of it, rather than allowing it to become a big issue between you? Hide the cap occasionally. Put foil or plastic wrap on the tube. Buy your own tube. Write on the mirror with the toothpaste. Approach minor discomforts creatively, not angrily!

On the other hand, if the well-being of others is involved, it's time to act. Maybe your community has created a safety hazard by ignoring a dangerous intersection; don't wait for someone else to take action. You could save a life by being the first to call the situation to attention.

3. What is the probability that you'll get what you want?

Is the change you want even possible? Is the other person likely to pay attention to your assertive action? Are you trying to "teach a lesson" that won't likely be learned anyway? Can you make it clear what you want? What's in it for the other person to do what you want?

If your boss doesn't give clear instructions, you'll want to let her know. When you do, however, *you* are going to have to be clear in your feedback. By telling her exactly what you need to know in order to fulfill her assignments to you, you'll make it more likely that she'll pay attention and give you what you need. And she knows that's in her best interest as well.

4. ARE YOU LOOKING FOR A SPECIFIC OUTCOME, OR JUST TO EXPRESS YOURSELF?

Can you express what you want in the form of a tangible change in the other person's behavior? Is there any actual *measurable* change you want to happen? Do you even want something to change, or do you just want recognition of your position?

When your local paper runs a story full of errors — and they all do from time to time — are you moved to let them know about it? If you write a letter to the editor, is it your goal to let your neighbors know how smart you are, or do you want the paper to run a correction so everyone has the facts? The tone of your letter will tell.

5. WHAT ARE YOUR OPTIONS?

Let's see . . . You can choose to go along and say nothing. You can speak up "softly." You can voice a firm objection. You can shout your feelings. You can write a letter (to someone involved, to a responsible agency, to the editor, to the president of the company, . . .). You can do some research and present your view of the real facts to everyone involved. If it's a public matter, you can organize a group of people to express an opinion in any of several ways.

It's likely that you really do have some choices in the matter. But not always. Sometimes there is simply nothing you can do.

6. ARE YOU LOOKING FOR A POSITIVE OUTCOME?

Is your goal in acting assertively likely to benefit everyone concerned? Are you trying for the greatest good for the greatest number, or just for yourself? Might your assertion make things worse?

Let's assume you live in a relatively small town, in which one large company is the biggest employer. You work there yourself, and you know the firm mistreats its employees. Wages are low (you know, because you have friends who work in the same industry elsewhere), benefits are the minimum required by law, sexual harassment by management is widespread, safety hazards are common. Can this be allowed to go on? Can it be improved? Isn't a "whistleblower" likely to be fired? Tough questions, and loaded with consequences, whatever you do. (We would encourage you to act, of course, but we don't have to live with the possible results of that action: firing, layoffs, plant closure, legal action, . . .) Here's where your careful consideration of the issues raised in this chapter will really pay off.

7. DO YOU HAVE ASSERTIVE ATTITUDE, SKILLS, INTENT . . . ?

Are you prepared to act in an appropriately assertive way? Have you practiced with less important assertions? Have you taken into account any special circumstances that will influence the situation? (e.g., cultural differences, physical or emotional disabilities, age differences . . .)

8. HAVE YOU COUNTED TO TEN?

Have you taken at least a few moments to reflect on the situation? Have you defused your angry feelings? Are you ready to express your concern rationally? Have you counted to ten — ten times? Have you worked on the anger material in chapter 14?

Consider what happens when you're behind the wheel of your car. Driving is a challenging test of skills these days, and not just skills of handling an automobile, either! The highways stretch one's patience, foresight, and ability to keep things in perspective. You'll inevitably come across others who appear less skilled than you consider yourself to be. The all-too-common impulse is to raise a protest, maybe an unheard shout to yourself and/or your passengers, and/or a hand-and-arm movement intended to be seen by the other driver. Don't! This is a classic opportunity to practice the "count-to-ten" maxim. It's virtually impossible to do anything which will *change* whatever happened. Anything you do after the fact will *not* "teach the other guy a lesson." And your action may endanger yourself and others on the road. This is one to let go.

9. Would it be better to wait until tomorrow?

Will you see the situation any more clearly if some time passes? Will the other person be more receptive later? Are you less likely to make a scene? Are there others around who should not see the confrontation?

Let's say your mother-in-law has been visiting for three days. This afternoon she returned from a shopping excursion with four new (and very ugly, in your opinion) throw pillows. She promptly spreads them around your living room, saying, "There! This place really needed brightening up, don't you think?" Ask yourself the questions above, and consider if this is the time to react.

10. Will you kick yourself if you don't take action?

Will it really matter to you tomorrow if you don't do something today? What's the worst thing that will happen if you do nothing? Will taking action help you feel better? Improve your self-concept?

You're enrolled in a college class which emphasizes student participation and class discussion. The teacher regularly mispronounces your name. You're both amused and offended by the error, but would like to have your classmates know the correct pronunciation (admittedly a difficult one). Here's a good chance to practice your assertive skills! (Hint: don't make the point in front of the class — at least not the first time.)

11. Have you done everything you can to remove or reduce the obstacles to your desired outcome?

Is there anything you can do to make the change you want easier for the other person? Are you willing and able to give as much as you get? Did you ask for clarification of her intent? Hieronymous, your neighbor's wolfhound, poops on your lawn regularly. You're tired of cleaning up after the mutt, but you don't want to create a neighborhood row, either. What to do? How about starting by taking a few steps yourself to prevent the problem? A fence, perhaps? Or one of the many sprays that discourage unwanted pet visits? If and when you do decide to discuss the problem with your neighbor, go armed with suggestions, and evidence that you're meeting him halfway, rather than simply demanding action on his part.

12. WHAT ARE THE PROBABLE CONSEQUENCES AND REALISTICS RISKS FROM YOUR POSSIBLE ASSERTION?

Might you or someone else be physically or emotionally hurt? Lose a job? Lose a relationship? What is the probability that the other person may become violent? Do you *know* the other person? Would your assertion provoke a confrontation? Will your assertion encroach on him/her in some way? Is he/she a reasonable person? Is pride a factor? Money? A romantic relationship? Public face-saving (e.g., with peers)?

If you're like most parents, discovering that a neighborhood bully beats up your child on the way home from school is a recurring nightmare. When it happens, your fear turns to anger and you want to take retaliatory action. But what? Beat up the bully? Beat up the bully's father? Tell the police? Call a neighborhood meeting? Arm your child with karate lessons? Visit with the bully's parents? Escort your child to and from school? Move? Hire a bodyguard?

Times such as this are a challenging test of judgement as well as assertive skills. Consider well your options and proceed with caution.

13. WILL ASSERTION MAKE ANY DIFFERENCE? WILL IT CHANGE THE SITUATION?

After all is said and done, how likely is it that anything will have changed? Will the change really be an improvement?

Perhaps you don't have a lot of confidence that your Congressperson does a very good job of representing your views and those of your neighbors in the local district. Maybe you've written letters, or called the office to express your opinions. Is it worth it to do more? Will it make a difference? Is your representative responsive to local needs, or is he/she governed by higher ambitions?

On the other hand, what about the local school board? Might you be able to make a difference there by paying attention to issues in your community and offering selected recommendations? Especially if you've been involved in community and/or school activities.

Choose the targets of your assertions so you get the most "bang for the buck" from your investment of time and energy.

DECIDING WHEN TO BE ASSERTIVE

1. Do you know what really happened?
2. How much does it matter?
3. Will you get what you want?
4. Do you just want to express yourself?
5. What are your options?
6. Do you want a positive outcome?
7. Are you prepared to be assertive?
8. Have you counted to ten?
9. Would it be better to wait?
10. Will you kick yourself if you do nothing?
11. Have you done everything you can?
12. What are the probable consequences — and risks?
13. Will assertion make any difference?

20

Helping Others Deal
with the New Assertive You

All paths lead to the same goal:
to convey to others what we are.
— PABLO NERUDA

A S YOU HAVE GROWN IN YOUR OWN ASSERTIVENESS, you have noticed changes in those around you. Your family, friends, co-workers and others may have found it strange to notice that you have changed, and they may not be altogether happy about it.

Most folks like to be able to predict how others will act in a given situation . . .

"Mom's not going to like that!"

"You'll really get it when your father gets home!"

"The boss is going to hit the ceiling!"

"Jim will really be pleased."

. . . and usually will express surprise if their expectations are not met . . .

"Why is Mary acting so differently these days?"

"What's gotten into George?"

"It's not like you to say something like that."

"You never used to mind if I borrowed your . . . !"

Your growing assertiveness will have some direct effects upon those closest to you. They may be glad to see you behaving more effectively; however, they may find it uncomfortable that you have begun to talk back, or to deny them full control in certain situations. You can prepare them for the changes in you; it will make a difference in how well they will support you in your growth.

How Does It Look from Outside?

"What's going on with Harold recently? He's been acting very strangely. I asked him if I could borrow his car, and he actually said no!"

People will notice. They'll wonder why you are no longer a pushover, or a grump. Some will applaud the changes, others will decry them — but they'll notice. It's common for students of assertiveness to overdo it at first. That makes the changes even more noticeable. Others may see you as suddenly *aggressive,* and you may be. If you are saying no for the first time in your life, you may get a kick out of really belting it out. "NO — and don't ask me again!"

If you overreact like that, and flaunt your newfound self-expression, others will resent it. Not only are you no longer predictable, you are a royal pain in the neck! From the point of view of your friends and family, you may appear to be a pushy so-and-so — one they'd just as soon would go away.

If instead, you're too tentative about your assertions, others may notice that something is changed, but not realize what you are trying to do.

It may be a good idea to let those closest to you know what you are trying to do — at least those you can trust — and perhaps even to ask them for help. Becoming assertive will involve your friends eventually if you are successful — there is no reason to hide it from those who could help you along the way. More on this later in the chapter.

BE AWARE OF YOUR IMPACT ON OTHERS

You will need to develop some sensitivity to the reactions of others to your assertion. You can teach yourself to observe the effects and to watch for the subtle clues others will give to their reactions.

Many of the same non-verbal behaviors we have stressed in assertive expression are involved. You've learned to pay attention to your own eye contact, posture, gestures, facial expression, voice, distance. . . . Tune in to the same characteristics in your listeners, to help you know how you are coming across, and how they are responding.

POTENTIAL ADVERSE REACTIONS

In our experience with helping others to learn assertiveness for more than two decades, we have found few negative results. Certain people do, however, respond in a disagreeable manner when they face assertion. Therefore, even if the assertion is handled properly — neither nonassertively nor aggressively to any degree — one may at times be faced with unpleasant reactions. Here are a few examples:

Backbiting. After you have asserted yourself, the other person involved may be somewhat disgruntled, though perhaps not openly. For example, if you see someone pushing her grocery cart into the line ahead of you and you respond assertively, she may go to the end of the line, but grumble while passing you. You may hear such things as "Who do you think you are, anyway?" "Big deal!" and so forth. We think the best solution is simply to ignore the childish behavior. If you do retort in some manner, you are likely only to complicate the situation by acknowledging that the words got to you.

Aggression. At times the other party may become outwardly hostile toward you. Yelling or screaming could be involved, or physical reactions like bumping, shoving, or hitting. Again, the best approach is to avoid escalating the condition. You may choose to express regret that she is upset by your actions, but remain steadfast in your assertion. This is especially true if you will have further contacts. If you back down on your assertion, you will simply reward this negative reaction, and the next time you assert yourself with this person the probability will be high that you will receive another aggressive reaction.

Temper Tantrums. In certain situations, you may assert yourself with someone who is used to being in charge. Such a person may react to your assertion by looking hurt, claiming precarious health, saying "You don't like me!" crying, feeling sorry for himself, or otherwise attempting to control you or make you feel guilty. Again, you must choose, but it is nearly always best to ignore such behavior.

Psychosomatic Reactions. Actual physical illness may occur in some individuals if you thwart a long-established habit. Abdominal pains, headaches, and feeling faint are just a few of the symptoms possible. Choose to be firm in the assertion, recognizing that the other person will adjust to the new situation in a short time. Be sure to be consistent in your assertion whenever the same situation recurs with this individual. If you are inconsistent, the other person may become confused and may eventually just ignore your assertions.

Overapologizing. On rare occasions after you have asserted yourself, the other party involved will be overly apologetic or humble to you. You should point out that such behavior is unnecessary. If, in later encounters she seems to be afraid of you or deferent toward you, do not take advantage. You could help to develop assertiveness in such a person, using the methods you have learned in this book.

Revenge. If you have a continuing relationship with someone with whom you have asserted yourself, that person may seek revenge. At first, it might be difficult to understand what is being attempted; but as time goes on the taunts may become quite evident. Once you are certain that someone is trying to make your life miserable, take steps to squelch the actions immediately. Directly confronting the situation is usually enough to get vengeful tactics to cease.

How Can You Include Others in Your Learning Process?

We suggested earlier in this chapter that you consider involving your most trusted friend(s) in your work on assertiveness. Try these steps:

. . . Tell your closest friend — be sure this is someone you can trust — that you are learning to be more assertive.

. . . Keep in mind that you will need to be careful when telling certain people about your attempts to become assertive. Those who have your best interests at heart will be supportive. Others — even some close friends and intimates — may actually undermine your efforts. Choose carefully.

. . . Tell your friend something about what it means to you to be assertive, and the differences between assertion and aggression.

. . . Ask your friend if she will help you.

. . . If she agrees, decide together on some specific behaviors she can watch for, and ask her to give you periodic feedback on how you are doing in those specifics — particularly the non-verbal components of behavior (chapter 7).

. . . Recognize that sometimes your assertiveness will lead you to say no to your friend, or otherwise say or do something against her preferences. Discuss that with her in advance and as it occurs.

. . . Avoid announcing, "I'm going to be assertive now!" — as if that excuses rudeness or other inappropriate behavior, or allows you to avoid responsibility for your actions.

. . . If you are developing your assertiveness as a part of some form of therapy, you need not disclose that to anyone. Simply talk about your goals, and point out that you are learning from this book.

. . . If you are working with a therapist or other trainer, you may wish to bring your friend in for an orientation/training session.

. . . If you decide to go ahead and let a friend in on your plans, you may find the statement on pages 210-211 useful in orienting that person to the assertiveness training process. Feel free to copy it, so long as you include the credit line at the bottom.

HOW A FRIEND CAN HELP

Someone has trusted you enough to ask for your help.

A friend, relative, roommate, coworker, lover or significant other has asked you to read this brief statement because he or she has decided to make some changes. The process your friend is pursuing is called assertiveness training (AT), and its purpose is to help folks become more capable in expressing themselves.

Assertiveness is often confused with aggressiveness, so let's clear that up right now. Learning to be more assertive does not mean learning to push other folks around in order to get your way. It does mean standing up for yourself, expressing feelings directly and firmly, establishing equal relationships which take the needs of both people into account.

Your friend may be reading a book, taking a class, working with a counselor, practicing alone or in a group — there are lots of ways AT can be effective. It may take a few weeks, or even a few months, but you'll begin to notice some changes. Your friend may be expressing opinions about where to go out to eat, what's wrong with the government, how you clean up your half of the apartment . . . maybe saying no when you ask a favor . . . taking more initiative in conversation . . . giving more compliments than before . . . or even showing anger once in a while. Not to worry. If these new actions were intended to threaten you, your friend would not have asked you to read this!

Most people find that increased assertiveness makes folks even more pleasant to be around. They're more spontaneous, less inhibited, more honest and direct, feel better about themselves, maybe even healthier!

So . . . how do you figure into this?

Well, your friend has asked you to read this so you'll know a little about what's going on in her or his life right now, and better understand the changes you may be seeing in the coming weeks and months.

You are evidently a trusted person in your friend's life, because it can be risky to let someone know about changes one plans to make. Sort of like telling people about your dreams, or your New Year's resolutions. If things don't work out, the person is vulnerable to some real hurt. Please honor the trust that has been extended to you.

Here are some ways you can help . . .

. . . find out something about how your friend hopes to change, so you'll know what to look for.

. . . when you see the desired changes — however small — give him a pat on the back.

. . . be honest in your own dealings with your friend . . . including pointing out when she goes overboard trying to be assertive.

. . . read up on assertiveness yourself.

. . . actively coach your friend with specific behavior changes, such as improved eye contact or voice tone.

. . . be a good model of assertiveness yourself.

. . . help your friend rehearse special situations, such as job interviews, or confrontations.

You'll likely find your thoughtfulness repaid manyfold. You may find yourself learning a thing or two in the process!

21

Beyond Assertiveness

God, give us the serenity to accept
what cannot be changed,
the courage to change
what should be changed,
and the wisdom to distinguish
one from the other.
  — REINHOLD NIEBUHR*

O
UR THEMES THROUGHOUT THIS BOOK have been *individual choice* and *equality in relationships*. While we have consistently pointed out the value of assertive behavior, perceptive readers will have recognized some of the potential shortcomings and hazards inherent in personal assertiveness. Sensitivity is required in taking into account some of these limitations and potentially negative consequences of asserting yourself.

Although assertive behavior will most often be its own reward, the consequences on occasion may deflate its value. Consider, for example, the young boy who assertively refuses the big bully's request to ride his new bike, and as a result finds himself nursing a black eye! His assertion was perfectly legitimate, but the other guy was unwilling to take no for an answer.

---

* Scholars now disagree about the origin of this prayer, but Niebuhr is generally credited with this specific version.

We certainly don't mean to suggest that assertiveness should be avoided if it appears hazardous, but we do encourage you to consider the probable *consequences* of your assertive acts. Under certain circumstances, the value of an assertion will be outweighed by the value of avoiding the probable response!

Sometimes with adults the reaction is more subtle than that of the street bully. Arlene found herself alienated from friends of twenty years when she criticized the way they were "spoiling" their son. It was nearly a year before the wound was healed. Meanwhile, Arlene wondered if the assertion really had been worth it.

If you *know how* to act assertively, you are free to *choose* whether or not you will. If you are *unable* to act assertively, you have no choices; you will be governed by others, and your well-being will suffer. *Our most important goal for this book is to enable YOU to make the choice!*

WHEN YOU ARE WRONG

Especially in your early assertions, you may assert yourself when you have incorrectly interpreted a situation. Also, you may assert yourself with a poor style and offend the other person. If either of these situations does occur, don't hesitate to admit that you have been wrong. There is no need to get carried away in making amends, of course; but be open enough to indicate that you know when you have been mistaken. And don't hesitate to be assertive with that person in the future when the situation calls for it.

"IT'S TOO LATE NOW!"

We are often asked about past situations by people who feel they can do nothing about a problem that happened some time ago. Frustrated by the consequences of their earlier lack of assertion, they nevertheless feel helpless to change the situation now.

Charlene, a busy executive, often completed letters and reports late in the day, and wound up asking George, her secretary, to stay late so he could type and duplicate the work for meetings the following morning. The first time, George assumed that the request was due to unique circumstances at that time. He willingly agreed to help out. Later, he found the "special request" had become an *expectation,* and occurred two or three times a week. Although he enjoyed the work, it interfered with his personal life, and he began to think of quitting the job.

George sought help in an assertiveness training group, where he somewhat tentatively brought the situation up for discussion. He found the trainer and group members very supportive. Selecting a relatively assertive woman in the group, he "rehearsed" with her a scene in which he confronted Charlene with his feelings. He did poorly at first, apologizing and allowing the "boss" to convince him that such "loyalty to the company" was necessary to the job. With feedback and support from the group, however, George improved his ability to express his feelings effectively and not be cowed by the executive's response.

The next day, George confronted Charlene at the office, made his point, and arranged a more reasonable schedule for such projects. In the two months that followed, she made "special requests" only twice, and only when the circumstances clearly were unusual. Both were pleased with the result.

The point of this discussion is that it is seldom too late for an appropriate assertion, even if a situation has grown worse over some time. Approaching the person involved — yes, even a family member, spouse, lover, boss, employee — with an honest "I've been concerned about . . . for some time" or "I've been wanting to talk with you about . . ." can lead to a most productive effort at resolution of an uncomfortable issue. And it can encourage open and honest communication in the future.

Keep in mind the importance of stating your feelings in such a way as to accept responsibility for them: "I'm concerned . . ." *not* "You've made me upset . . ."; "I'm mad . . ." *not* "You make me mad . . ."

Another important reason to go back and take care of old business with others is that unfinished business continues to gnaw away at you. Resentment from experiences which created anger or hurt won't just go away. Such feelings result in a widening gap between people, and the resulting mistrust and potential grudge are hurtful to both persons.

Even if the old issues cannot be amicably resolved, doing all you can to *attempt* reconciliation is a very healthy and worthwhile step for you. We recognize that opening up old wounds can be painful. And there are certain risks — the outcomes *could* be worse than before. Despite these risks, we have seen so many people gain great rewards from resolving old conflicts that we do not hesitate to encourage you to do all you can to work out any such problems in your own life.

One more point: As we have cautioned before, do not attempt to *begin* your journey toward new assertiveness with highly risky relationships — those which are very important to you. This is a rather advanced step, and should come after you have mastered the basics.

THE SWING OF THE PENDULUM

> *"I have this friend who went through assertiveness training and now is unbearable! This person, who used to be peaceful and quiet, is complaining about everything. She has really gone overboard! Isn't assertiveness training dangerous at times because it creates monsters?"*

People who have considered themselves underdogs throughout life, and then learned to be assertive, do often move beyond assertion into verbal aggressiveness. The message may be, "Now I've got my chance, and I'll set a few people straight!" Feelings held down or covered up for so many years often come out with a "bang" when new skills for self-expression are learned.

The converse of this situation may also be true: Those who have been prone to aggressive behavior, such as manipulation, may go overboard when first learning to be assertive, becoming overly sensitive and responsive to people. It can be flabbergasting to suddenly be treated like a queen or king by someone who was formerly derisive and calculating!

Both of these dramatic shifts in behavior are normal reactions and to be expected under the circumstances. The pendulum was "stuck." Now released, the person seeks to experience the full range of behavior. We suggest patience in these instances. The pendulum will swing back after a relatively brief period of experimentation, and assertion will be accepted eventually as the best alternative.

ASSERTIVENESS IN A HOLISTIC PERSPECTIVE

Assertiveness training is a valuable tool for gaining self-confidence and self-control in life, but it is not a cure-all. AT works best when used along with other ways to get healthy. We advocate a holistic-eclectic approach, integrating a variety of psychological methods with physical, spiritual and environmental considerations. It is vital to deal with all parts of yourself.

Take a look at your total self. Medical history, current medical condition, dietary and physical exercise patterns, spiritual strengths and weaknesses, living conditions — are all important considerations in a thorough assessment of well-being. Do not assume that a lack of assertiveness, for example, will be adequately dealt with by an AT program alone. The problem could be largely dietary! Examine all the possibilities, and engage medical and/or spiritual professionals as well if you need their help.

The historic roots of holistic procedures are traceable to ancient Egypt. The modern regeneration of these concepts has been stimulated by such factors as increased consumer activism, exorbitant health care costs, the women's movement, and the assertiveness movement. Despite the continuing tendency for specialization, an increasingly holistic outlook is emerging among health professionals in all fields.

ASSERT YOUR WAY TO HEALTH

Can lack of assertive behavior make you sick?

Recent studies in two relatively new fields of mind-body relationships: behavioral medicine and — get ready — *psychoneuroimmunology* (whew), suggest that deficiencies in assertiveness can play an important role in developing and treating illnesses.

Patients who have such ailments as AIDS, cancer, heart disease, respiratory problems, gastrointestinal tract disorders, and arthritis are being studied by medical researchers to determine if stress factors related to long-term non-assertive or aggressive behavior contribute to bringing on the illness. The relationship between mind and body is complex, of course, and interpretations about the causes of illness need to be tentative. Responsible researchers observe that the cause of illness is rarely a single factor such as assertiveness problems or smoking, but a variety of factors working together.

Cardiologist Redford Williams, whom we introduced in the Anger chapter, is one of those researchers. He has studied the role of hostility as a causative factor in cardiovascular disease. Numerous studies by Williams and his colleagues at Duke University point to hostile attitudes and behaviors as an important risk factor in heart attacks, right along with the key physical risk factors of smoking, elevated blood cholesterol, and high blood pressure.

Williams recommends assertiveness training as one part of his multi-faceted treatment program to reduce hostility and other risk factors. He has found that the more you can deal with your feelings in an upfront, straightforward manner, the less you allow feelings to fester and come out as hostile or cynical thoughts and behaviors.

Another way to use your assertive skills to improve your health is to take charge of your own healthcare. That even means learning to be assertive when you must go to the doctor. Researchers in the mind-body field are teaching patients how to do it. Internist Sheldon Greenfield and social psychologist Sherrie Kaplan have devised a 20-minute assertiveness coaching session for patients waiting to see a physician. They rehearsed how to ask key questions in order to take an active role in the process of dealing with the doctor.

Greenfield and Kaplan found, when they compared these patients with a group of patients who had not been trained, that the coached assertiveness patients were much more in control in dealing with the doctor. They directed the conversation, interrupted when necessary, and got a lot more information about their illnesses.

And here's the great part . . . four months later those trained in assertiveness had missed less work, had fewer medical symptoms, and indicated that their overall health was better than the uncoached patients.

There are many ways to be an assertive advocate in your own healthcare program before and after you become ill. Believing in and taking action about your ongoing healthcare is assertive behavior. Educate yourself about your total self: body-mind-spirit. Do ongoing preventative maintenance in terms of low-fat, well-balanced diet, an aerobic exercise program, and working on your psychological and spiritual health.

The bottom line is learning to be in charge of your own life and healthcare. Get better at making important decisions about: the doctors you select and how you deal with them; your health insurance coverage and how claims are handled; educating yourself and your illness and treatment; dealing with doctor's office and hospital personnel; decision making in regard to medications and alternative treatments. All of these are vital areas of concern in an assertive approach to your healthcare. You are not only protecting your rights, you are protecting your life.

We urge you to develop an assertive lifestyle, and to take care of yourself, holistically!

ASSERTIVENESS AND COMMON SENSE

We've emphasized action in this book. When we first began to do assertiveness training back in the late 1960s, we found it an effective procedure for our clients who had difficulty expressing themselves. Most of them were shy, nonassertive, reluctant to take any action on their own behalf. For them, it seemed the most effective approach was to *activate* them, to get them going again, to teach them to "stand up, speak out, and talk back." Moreover, assertiveness was a very helpful intervention for those who were inhibited by social anxiety.

Later we came to recognize that many people were using the idea of taking such action as a license to act aggressively, or at least foolishly. Some trainers were advocating — as homework in assertiveness — that people go into restaurants and ask just for a glass of water. Or into service stations and ask just to have the windows washed (in those days service stations actually did that sort of thing!).

Let us put in a plea, then, for common sense:

Don't Manipulate. Assertiveness goes a long way, when used appropriately. But it ought not be used as a tool for manipulation, or as a means to "get your way" at the expense of others (aggressive), or as a constant style of behavior.

Don't Get in a Rut. You need not "assert yourself" all the time. How boring, — and boorish — to go about always making yourself heard, always speaking out. Make assertiveness one tool in your repertoire of behaviors, one way to act which you can use when it is important and needed. Nothing is good all the time! There is such a thing as "too much of a good thing!"

Be Kind. Kindness is a word we are hearing more about these days. It has been our intent since the beginning of our work with assertiveness to help humans treat each other with respect, thoughtfulness, and yes, kindness. The idea of assertiveness for those who had been "pushed around" earlier was to help them gain the respect that they had been missing from others.

Assertiveness is *not* incompatible with kindness, thoughtfulness, compassion, empathy, politeness. A truly assertive lifestyle is very concerned for others, and their rights. The term "empathic assertion" has been used to describe those forms of self-expression which are directly aimed at the needs of another person.

We're in full support of the "random kindness" movement, and especially like Dr. Gavin Whitsett's "guerilla kindness" ideas: do acts of kindness anonymously, without possibility of recognition or reward.

Be Yourself. An unfortunate number of people have interpreted assertiveness as a monolithic concept — as if there were one single definition which qualified a behavior as "assertive." We discussed this at some length in chapter 5, but we'd like to underscore it here by encouraging recognition of individual differences.

Everybody has a unique view of the world; that is part of the joy of the human experience. Don't try to shape others into your image of them! Don't assume there is only one way to be assertive in a given circumstance! Let people choose to be non-assertive if they wish. Let there be "different strokes for different folks!"

Be Persistent — But Not a Pest. One of the most important but often overlooked aspects of assertive behavior is persistence. It is rarely enough just to ask for what you want. You may need to ask again, to direct your request to someone in authority, to write a letter, to bring some pressure to bear from another source (a consumer advocacy group, a regulatory agency). . . .

Is your cause important? Go back again if you don't get help the first time. See the manager. Call the president of the company. Tell your neighbor again about his noisy dog. Remind your boss about the raise.

Remember to be assertive in your persistence — nagging can be aggressive!

Practice — But Don't Get "Perfect." Some types of so-called "assertive" responses can seem really mechanical and rehearsed. While we advocate that you rehearse while you are developing your style and skills in assertiveness, we consider it very important that you develop a personal style — integrating assertiveness with your own unique way of dealing with people. If you come off sounding like our book, or like someone else's "scripts for assertive situations" you'll lose credibility, and people will not take you seriously.

Forget about Being an Amateur Shrink. Don't try to psychoanalyze people! Some folks go around trying to "think psychologically," always figuring out how others are likely to react, and shaping their behavior by the way they believe it will affect others. It is rare that anyone — even those of us who are trained psychologists — is able to do that successfully.

Instead, try to be yourself, be assertive, and take other's needs, rights, and respect into account.

MEMBERSHIP IN THE HUMAN COMMUNITY

Thornton Wilder, in his classic play, *Our Town,* addressed one of his key characters thus: "Jane Crofeet, the Crofeet Farm, Grover's Corners, Sutton County, New Hampshire, United States of America, Continent of North America, the Earth, the Solar System, the Universe, the Mind of God." Wilder showed a remarkable sense of citizenship in the world; few of us have so thoughtfully considered our relationships to the entire human community.

Indeed, is it even possible to deal with that virtually unreachable concept? In what sense *am* I a world citizen? I can talk with and see my neighbors in the local community. I can visit, with minimal difficulty, people in nearby states, or even across the country, and, if I am fortunate, around the world. I can share government agencies; vote in local, state and national elections; share a historical and cultural heritage with other citizens of the United States. What have I in common with the people of Namibia, or Lithuania, or Sri Lanka? Do I really think of them as my brothers and sisters in humankind?

No individual can exist alone. None of us has the necessary knowledge, skills, or personal resources necessary to function with total independence in the world. We are interdependent, and our assertiveness must take into account and respect our neighbors' needs as well as our own.

Even without the evidence offered by photos from space, it's easy to see the fragility of world order in any day's headlines. We note the continuing efforts by governments of many nations to maintain world peace and some balance of order on the planet. And we see how easily aggression and the quest for power disturb that balance.

So many international issues remain unresolved, awaiting assertive action by those courageous enough to transcend nationalistic limits and assume leadership in *solving problems,* rather than displaying power. Hunger, extreme poverty, sanitation, disposal of nuclear and other hazardous wastes . . . the list goes on.

The principles of assertive action which we have discussed throughout this book apply to these concerns as well. Perhaps you have found assertiveness training helpful in your own life and relationships. We urge you to demonstrate your appreciation for that help by taking assertive action as a world citizen. Write letters supporting public officials who take courageous action.

Contact your elected representatives to express your views on important issues.

Work to replace aggression with assertion wherever you can. You may choose to support tighter controls on handguns, for instance, or reduced television violence. Some will demonstrate against nuclear power plants or weapons proliferation. Perhaps you advocate free-enterprise replacement of government bureaucracies which fail to provide necessary services. Equal justice for women or minorities may be your major cause. Support is always needed for local programs of rape crisis intervention, and training for parents to help them protect their children.

The principle of assertive action is well established in Western culture, and a vital element in the U.S. Constitution. The spirit of civil disobedience, when other attempts to change intolerable situations have failed, has a proud heritage. Henry David Thoreau is the "patron saint" of civil disobedience, but one need look no further than the U.S. Declaration of Independence or such famous historic events as the Boston Tea Party for other well known and highly respected foundations.

A vital principle of any such action, of course, is the individual's willingness to accept responsibility for the consequences thereof. Examples of such personally responsible, public assertiveness from the last century are Mahatma Ghandi, Martin Luther King, Desmond Tutu, and Lech Walesa. Whatever our personal views of the substantive issues in their actions, we must stand in awe of those who have made their deepest beliefs public by living accordingly, caring more for the welfare of humankind than for their individual comfort and safety. Who will we admire a hundred years from now?

Ultimately, those acts which are in the best interest of our fellow humans are in our own best interests as well. If I act assertively to right a social wrong, I act to the benefit of all who are members of the society, including myself. Thus assertive action, in the best sense, is at once in my own self-interest and unselfish!

There are a thousand causes worthy of your energies. If your assertiveness ends when your steak is served the way you like it, or when you get correct change, your life may be more pleasant temporarily, but will not count for much.

Justice Oliver Wendell Holmes put it in perspective (do forgive his sexist language):

> *"A man must share in the action and passion of his times, at the risk of being judged not to have lived."*

BEYOND ASSERTIVENESS
Enough. The rest is up to you.

Keep in mind:

. . . Assertiveness, as other social behavior, is learned. You can change yourself if you wish to do so.

. . . Change is hard work. It usually comes slowly, and in small steps. Don't try to tackle too much at once. Succeed by taking *achievable steps!*

. . . There are no magic answers. While assertiveness doesn't always work, (for us either!), it sure beats the alternatives — nearly all the time! Don't let failures at first stop you from trying again.

. . . Give yourself credit when you bring about changes in your life. Even the smallest accomplishments deserve a pat on the back!

. . . Don't hesitate to ask for help — including professional help when you need it. Everyone needs help at times.

. . . You are working with an infinitely valuable resource — yourself. Take good care!

You are unique, an individual, with your own size, shape, color, age, ethnic and cultural background, sex, lifestyle, education, ideas, values, occupation, relationships, thoughts, behavior patterns. In this book we have had to generalize a great deal. Assertiveness training cannot be all things to all people. *You* must decide what is relevant for you. If you choose to use AT as a tool to help you become the person you want to be, you must also decide how to apply its principles to your own unique life situation.

Remember that assertiveness is *not* a tool for manipulation, or intimidation, or getting your way. It is a means to stand up for your own rights, to build equal relationships, to express your anger, to reach out to others, to express your affection, to be more direct. Most importantly, it is one means to become the person you want to be, to feel good about yourself, and to demonstrate your caring and respect for the rights of others.

Appendices

APPENDIX A

Assertiveness Practice Situations

The everyday life situations which follow call for assertive behavior, and cause difficulty for many people. Each situation is presented with alternatives from which you may choose a response. Each alternative response may be categorized in the "nonassertive-aggressive-assertive" framework we have described.

The situations are designed for your practice according to the step-by-step process described in chapter 12. Pick situations appropriate to your needs, and work slowly, on one item at a time. As you read the situation description, fill in the details from your own imagination.

Follow steps 4 to 7 of chapter 12, utilizing the alternative responses suggested here for each situation, and any others you may think of. For each situation you choose, enact the role-playing and feedback exercises described in Steps 8, 9, 11 and 12; then continue with remaining steps of the step-by-step process. Remember to focus both upon what you say, and *how* you say it!

The examples are grouped according to several characteristic types of situations: family, intimate, consumer, employment, school and community, and social. In each case, only a few situations are suggested, although the number of categories and examples is as infinite as life itself. We urge you to come up with more examples of your own to extend your practice.

FAMILY SITUATIONS

Sleepover. Your 12-year-old daughter is having a sleepover with five other girls. It is past 2 a.m.; the girls should have settled down to sleep by now, but they're still making a lot of noise.
Alternative Responses:
    a) You toss and turn in bed, wishing your spouse would get up and say something to the girls. You're really angry, but just lie there trying to block out the sounds.

b) You jump out of bed and scold the girls angrily, especially your daughter, for their behavior.

c) You get up, speak to the girls firmly (so they know you mean business), and tell them you've had enough for tonight. You point out that you need to get up early tomorrow, and that everyone needs to get to sleep. You make clear that you won't tolerate any more noise.

Visiting Relative. Aunt Margaret, with whom you'd really rather not spend much time, is on the telephone, telling you of her plans to arrive next week for a three week visit with you.
Alternative Responses:

a) You think, "Oh, no!" but say, "We'd love to have you come and stay as long as you like!"

b) You tell her the children have just come down with bad colds, the roof is leaking, and you'll be going to Cousin Bill's weekend after next — none of which is true.

c) You say, "We'll be glad to have you come for the weekend, but we simply can't invite you for longer. A short visit is happier for everyone, and we'll want to see each other again sooner. We have lots of school and community activities which take up most of our evenings and weekends."

Past Midnight. Your teenage son has just returned from a school party. It's 3 a.m., and you've been frantic, worried mainly if he was okay. You had expected him home before midnight.
Alternative Responses:

a) You turn over and go to sleep.

b) You shout, "Where the hell have you been? Do you have any idea what time it is? You've kept me up all night! You thoughtless, inconsiderate, selfish, no-good bum — I ought to make you sleep in the street!"

c) You say, "Are you okay, Sean? I've been very upset, worrying about you! You said you'd be home before midnight, and I've been frantic for hours. I wish you'd called me! Tomorrow we'll discuss your arrangements for staying out late."

Holy Terror. The pre-school teacher tells you that your son is hitting the other children. At home he "runs the show," staying up late, playing too rough with the pets, not eating properly. In the past you have thought his behavior "cute."
Alternative Responses:

a) You talk gently to your son about not hitting the other children. He says the other kids are mean, but that he is sorry. He jumps in your lap and you say, "You are such a sweet boy. I love you."

b) You grab your son roughly and say that if he hits anyone else you'll beat his bottom till it's raw.

c) You discuss the issue with the teacher and with your family physician. After ruling out any physical causes, you make an appointment with the non-profit family services center for counseling help.

INTIMATE SITUATIONS

Late for Dinner. Your wife was supposed to be home for dinner right after work. Instead, she returns hours later explaining she was out with the girls for a few drinks. She is obviously drunk.

Alternative Responses:

a) You say nothing about how thoughtless she has been, but simply start preparing something for her to eat.

b) Screaming and yelling, you tell her that she is a drunken fool, doesn't care about your feelings, is a poor example for the children. You ask about what the neighbors will think. You demand that she get her own dinner.

c) You calmly and firmly let her know that she should have informed you beforehand that she was going out and would likely be late. "At least you could have called me. Your cold dinner is in the kitchen. We'll discuss this more tomorrow." And you do.

Plastic Money. Finances are tight. When you receive the credit card bill for the month, you are shocked. Your spouse has charges that seem excessive and unnecessary.

Alternative Responses:

a) You go to the bank and cash a check for an equal amount of money and spend it on yourself in revenge. You don't mention the credit card.

b) You realize that you also have over-spent before. You still feel upset, but decide to be understanding this time.

c) You arrange an appropriate time to discuss the finances, and tell your partner that when you opened the statement, you were shocked at the charges. Asking for an explanation, you also insist that the two of you agree on some guidelines for use of the credit card.

Sagging Sex. During the past six months, your spouse has not been sexually attentive. You're having intercourse less often, and your spouse is not as enthusiastic or caring. You have tried harder to motivate your partner, but to no avail.

Alternative Responses:

a) You decide that two can play this game. You withdraw, complain to your friends, and criticize your spouse openly in front of the children about non-related matters.

b) The feelings of upset have built to a boiling point. One evening, after another dull sexual encounter, you lash out irrationally. Your spouse retaliates.

The verbal explosion lasts for hours. Still seething, you spend that night on the couch and the next week sulking.

c) In a non-inflammatory-but-firm style, you speak to your partner honestly and openly about your feelings. You suggest that you both take part in a couple's workshop or go see a counselor to work on the problem.

CONSUMER SITUATIONS

Haircut. At the barber shop, the barber has just finished cutting your hair. When he turns the chair toward the mirror so you can inspect, you notice that you'd like the sides trimmed more.
Alternative Responses:

a) You nod your head and say, "That's OK."

b) Abruptly you demand that he do a more thorough job, adding sarcastically, "You sure didn't take much off the sides, did you?"

c) You tell the barber you would like to have the sides trimmed more.

Short-changed. As you are leaving a store after a small purchase, you discover that you have been short-changed by three dollars.
Alternative Responses:

a) Pausing for a moment, you try to decide if $3 is worth the effort. After a few moments, you decide it is not and go on your way.

b) You hurry back into the store and loudly demand your money, making a derogatory comment about "cashiers who can't add."

c) Re-entering the store, you catch the attention of the clerk, saying that you were short-changed by three dollars. In the process of explaining, you display the change you received back, along with your receipt.

Waiting in Line. You are standing near a cash register waiting to pay for your purchase and have it wrapped. Others who have come after you are being waited on first. You are getting tired of waiting.
Alternative Responses:

a) You give up and decide not to buy the article.

b) Shouting, "You sure get poor service in this store!" you slam the intended purchase down on the counter and walk out.

c) In a voice loud enough to be heard, you tell the clerk "I'm next. I was ahead of people who have already been served. Please wait on me now."

Phone Blues. You are at home, hoping for a restful day. About 11 A.M., the phone rings, and the voice asks if you are (your name). The call sounds important. Then you hear. "This is *Rocky Road Magazine*. We're conducting a readership survey. Have you read *Rocky Road?*" You're perturbed at the intrusion.

Alternative Responses:

a) You are polite, don't interrupt and answer all of the caller's questions. Soon you hear a "sales pitch" instead of a "readership survey." The call lasts ten minutes.

b) You yell, "You people are a bunch of vultures! Don't you know anything about telephone privacy? Stick it in your ear!" You slam down the phone.

c) You state firmly, "I'm not interested." The caller replies, "I only want to ask you a few questions." You repeat firmly, "I'm not interested." You hang up the phone.

EMPLOYMENT SITUATIONS

Working Late. You and your partner have an engagement this evening which has been planned for several weeks. You plan to leave immediately after work. Mid-afternoon, however, your supervisor asks you to stay late this evening to work on a special assignment.

Alternative Responses:

a) You say nothing about your important plans and simply agree to stay until the work is finished.

b) In a nervous, abrupt voice you say, "No, I won't work late tonight! You're going to have to plan ahead!" You then turn back to your work.

c) In a firm, pleasant voice, you explain your important plans and say you will not be able to stay this evening to work on the special assignment, but perhaps you can help find an alternative solution. (If this is the first time you've been asked, you may also wish to volunteer to come in early in the morning to work on the project.)

Deniable Passion. One of your co-workers has been making sexual overtures toward you. You are not the least bit interested and have begun to feel harassed.

Alternative Responses:

a) You begin wearing clothing that is less appealing, change your hair style, and start looking away each time the person approaches.

b) The next time the person makes an overture you exclaim loudly, "You are scum! I hate being around you! Stay away from me or I'll report you to the harassment police!"

c) When the person next approaches you, you respond quietly but very firmly. You say that you have no interest in a relationship, and give examples of the person's unacceptable behavior. You state clearly that if the approaches don't stop, you will file a harassment complaint with your employer.

Below Par. An employee you supervise has been doing sub-standard work recently. You decide it is best to deal with the situation before it gets out of control.

Alternative Responses:

a) You say very quietly, "I'm sorry to bring this up, but I know you must have a good reason why your work has seemed to slide a little lately."

b) You shout, "What is it with you? You've been doing a lousy job lately. If you don't shape up pronto, you'll be out of here!"

c) You take the employee aside and say, "I am very concerned about your work performance recently. You haven't earned a pay increase this period. Let's analyze what's been going on and see what improvements you can make for the future."

Job Error. You've made a mistake on the job. Your supervisor discovers it and is coming down on you with extra-harsh criticism and a reprimand.
Alternative Responses:

a) Overapologizing, you say, "I'm sorry. It was stupid of me to be so careless. I'll never let it happen again! Please forgive me!"

b) You bristle and glare, saying, "Mind your own business! Where do you get off criticizing my work? Since when are you perfect? Leave me alone, and don't bother me in the future. I can handle my job!"

c) You acknowledge the mistake, saying, "I hear you, and I admit my mistake. I'll be more careful. I don't think there will be problems in the future, but if there are, I hope we can discuss them more calmly. I learn better from criticism that's not so harsh."

Late to Work. One of your subordinates has been coming in late consistently for the last three or four days.
Alternative Responses:

a) You grumble to yourself or to others about the situation, but say nothing to the person, hoping he will start coming in on time.

b) You tell the worker off loudly in front of the rest of the crew. You declare that he has no right to take advantage of you and that he'd better get to work on time or you'll see that he is fired.

c) You speak to the worker alone, noting that you've observed him coming in late recently. You ask, "Is there an explanation I should know about? If so, you should have told me, instead of leaving me up in the air. What needs to change so you can start coming to work on time?"

SCHOOL AND COMMUNITY SITUATIONS

Quiet Prof. In a lecture with 300 students, the professor speaks very softly. You're having trouble hearing him, and you know that many others are as well.
Alternative Responses:

a) You continue to strain to hear, eventually moving closer to the front of the room, but say nothing about his too-soft voice.

b) You yell out, "Speak up!"

c) You speak to the professor after class, point out the problem, and ask if he would please speak louder.

Clarification. At a Lion's Club meeting, the president is discussing the procedures for the annual high school speech contest. You're puzzled by several of his statements and believe he has incorrectly described the rules.

Alternative Responses:

a) You say nothing, but continue to mull over the question, looking up your notes from last year's contest later in the day.

b) You interrupt, telling him he is wrong, pointing out the mistake and correcting him from your own knowledge of the contest. Your tone is derisive, and your choice of words obviously makes him ill-at-ease.

c) You ask the president to explain the procedures further, expressing your confusion and noting the source of your conflicting information.

Morals. You are one of eleven people in a discussion group on human sexuality. The concepts being supported by three or four of the more verbal students are contrary to your personal moral code.

Alternative Responses:

a) You listen quietly, not disagreeing openly with the other members or describing your own views.

b) You loudly denounce the views which have been expressed. Your defense of your own beliefs is strong, and you urge others to accept your point of view as the only correct one.

c) You speak up in support of your own beliefs, taking an apparently unpopular position, but not putting down the beliefs of others in the group.

Know It All. As a member of the community beautification committee, you are dismayed by the continued dominance of group discussion by Ms. Brown, an opinionated member who has "the answer" to every question. She has begun another tirade, already lasting several minutes. As usual, no one has said anything about it..

Alternative Responses:

a) Your irritation increases, but you remain silent.

b) You explode verbally, curse Ms. Brown for "not giving anyone else a chance," and declare her ideas "out-of-date and worthless."

c) You interrupt, saying, "Excuse me, Ms. Brown; you're making some really good points, but I want you to know that I get irritated when you monopolize the group's time." Speaking directly to her as well as the other group members, you suggest a discussion procedure which will permit all members an opportunity to take part, and will minimize dominance by a single individual.

SOCIAL SITUATIONS

Breaking the Ice. At a party where you don't know anyone except the host, you want to circulate and get to know others. You walk up to three people talking.
Alternative Responses:

a) You stand close to them and smile but say nothing, waiting for them to notice you.

b) You listen to the subject they are talking about, then break in and disagree with someone's viewpoint.

c) You break into the conversation immediately and introduce yourself.

d) You wait for a pause in the conversation, then introduce yourself and ask if you may join in.

Making a Date. You'd like to ask out a person you've met and talked with three or four times recently.
Alternative Responses:

a) You sit around the telephone going over in your mind what you'll say and how your friend will respond. Several times you lift the phone and almost finish dialing, then hang up.

b) You phone and as soon as your friend answers, you respond by saying, "Hi, baby, we're going out together this weekend!" Taken aback, your friend asks, "Who's calling?"

c) You call, and when your friend answers, you identify yourself and ask, "How's school going?" The reply is, "Fine, except I'm worried about an econ test on Friday." Following the lead, you talk for a few minutes about the test. Then you say, "Since the big test will be over, would you like to go to a movie on Friday evening?"

Smoke Gets in Your Lungs. You're at a public meeting in the community park. A man you don't know sits down next to you, puffing enthusiastically on a large cigar. The smoke is very offensive to you.
Alternative Responses:

a) You suffer the offensive smoke in silence, deciding it is the right of the other person to smoke outdoors if he wishes.

b) You're very angry, and you demand that he either move or put out the cigar. You loudly attack the evils of smoking and the health hazards of second-hand smoke .

c) You firmly but politely ask him to refrain from smoking because it is offensive to you.

d) You ask him to move to another seat some distance away if he wants to continue smoking, since you were there first.

SUMMARY

We have covered a wide range of assertiveness situations in this appendix. We trust you'll find them valuable:

❖ To demonstrate that assertive behavior can be utilized in many areas of our lives.

❖ To show that the nonassertive-aggressive-assertive format is universal regardless of the specific situation involved.

❖ To prime your thinking about other situations in your life that need your assertive attention.

❖ To offer ideas about how to handle instances where assertive behavior is indicated.

You probably had no trouble seeing yourself in many of the examples. Chances are you recognized something of yourself in each of the responses. Remember that no one is assertive all the time. As you progress, you'll be nonassertive or aggressive less often, and you'll develop a more consistent and natural assertive style. But you won't become perfect! Even people who write books on assertiveness have trouble with nonassertive and aggressive behavior at times!

We wish you well.

APPENDIX B

References and
Further Reading

Adams, S. *The Dilbert Principle*. New York: HarperBusiness, 1997.

Alberti, R.E. and Emmons, M.L. *Assertiveness and Social Skills Training: A Practical Therapist Guide*. Atascadero, California: Impact Publishers, Inc., 2001.

Alberti, R.E. and Emmons, M.L. *Your Perfect Right: A Guide to Assertive Living*. Atascadero, California: Impact Publishers, Inc., 1970, 1974, 1978, 1982, 1986, 1990, 1995.

Alberti, R.E. and Emmons, M.L. *Your Perfect Right* (audiotape edition). Mission, Kansas: Skillpath Publications, 1999.

Beck, A. *Love Is Never Enough*. New York: HarperCollins, 1988.

Beck, A. *Prisoners of Hate: The Cognitive Basis of Anger, Hostility, and Violence*. New York: HarperCollins, 1999.

Bolles, R.N. *What Color Is Your Parachute?* Berkeley, California: Ten Speed Press, 2001 (annual).

Bourne, E. *The Anxiety and Phobia Workbook*. Oakland, California: New Harbinger, 1990.

Burns, D. *Feeling Good: The New Mood Therapy* (second edition). New York: William Morrow, 1999.

Cautela, J. and Groden, J. *Relaxation: A Comprehensive Manual For Adult, Children, And Children With Special Needs*. Champaign, IL: Research Press, 1994.

Cheek, D.K. *Assertive Black... Puzzled White*. San Luis Obispo, California: Author, 1976.

Cooley, M.L. and Hollandsworth, J.G. A Strategy for teaching verbal content of assertive responses. In R.E. Alberti (ed.) *Assertiveness: Innovations, Applications, Issues*. San Luis Obispo, California: Impact Publishers, Inc., 1977. (Now out of print, but available in many libraries.)

Davis, M., Eshelman, E., McKay, M. *The Relaxation and Stress Reduction Workbook.* New Harbinger Publications, 1980.

Elgin, S.H. *The Last Word on the Gentle Art of Verbal Self-Defense.* New York: Prentice Hall, 1987.

Ellis, A. *Feeling Better, Getting Better, Staying Better.* Atascadero, California: Impact Publishers, Inc. 2001.

Ellis, A. *How to Make Yourself Happy and Remarkably Undisturbable.* Atascadero, California: Impact Publishers, Inc. 1999.

Ellis, A. and Lange, A. *How to Keep People from Pushing Your Buttons.* New York: Carol PublishingGroup, 1994.

Emery, G. *Own Your Own Life.* New York: Signet, 1984.

Emmons, M.L. *The Inner Source: A Guide to Meditative Therapy.* San Luis Obispo, California: Author, 1978.

Emmons, M. and Richardson, D. *The Assertive Christian.* Minneapolis: Winston Press, 1981.

Fensterheim, H. and Baer, J. *Don't Say Yes When You Want To Say No.* New York: Dell, 1975.

Fisher, R., and Ury, W. *Getting to Yes: Negotiating Agreement Without Giving In.* New York: Penguin Books, 1983.

Friedman, M. *Type A Behavior – Its Diagnosis and Treatment.* New York: Plenum, 1996.

Fromm, E. *The Art of Loving.* New York: Harper and Row, 1956.

Gordon, T. *Parent Effectiveness Training.* New York: Wyden, 1970.

Greenberger, D. and Padesky, C.A. *Mind Over Mood: Changing the Way You Feel by Changing the Way You Think.* New York: The Guilford Press, 1995

Grohol, J. *The Insider's Guide to Mental Health Resources Online.* New York: Guilford Press, 2000 (annual updates).

Haney, M. and Boenisch, E. *The Stress Owner's Manual.* Atascadero, California: Impact Publishers, Inc., 1996.

Hunt, M. The lessons of the cliff. *Parade Magazine.* July 14, 1985.

Kottler, J.A. *Beyond Blame: A New Way of Resolving Conflicts in Relationships.* San Francisco: Jossey-Bass Publishers, 1994.

Lange, A.J. and Jakubowski, P. *The Assertive Option.* Champaign, Illinois: Research Press, 1978.

Lazarus, A.A. *Marital Myths Revisited.* Atascadero, California: Impact Publishers, Inc., 2001.

McKay, G. and Dinkmeyer, Sr., D. *How You Feel Is Up to You*. Atascadero, California: Impact Publishers, Inc., 1994.

Palmer, P. *Liking Myself*. San Luis Obispo, California: Impact Publishers, Inc., 1977. (Now out of print, but available in many libraries.)

Palmer, P. *The Mouse, The Monster & Me*. San Luis Obispo, California: Impact Publishers, Inc., 1977. (Now out of print, but available in many libraries.)

Palmer, P., and Froehner, M. *Teen Esteem: A Self-Direction Manual for Young Adults* (second edition). Atascadero, California: Impact Publishers, Inc., 2000.

Phelps, S. and Austin, N. *The Assertive Woman* (third edition). Atascadero, California: Impact Publishers, Inc., 1975, 1987, 1997.

Pogrebin, L.C. *Among Friends*. New York: McGraw-Hill, 1987.

Potter, S. *Three-Upmanship*. New York: Holt, Rinehart and Winston, 1962.

Rogers, C.R. *On Becoming a Person*. Boston: Houghton-Mifflin, 1961.

Salter, A. *Conditioned Reflex Therapy*. New York: Farrar, Straus, and Giroux, 1949 (Capricorn Books edition, 1961).

Satir, V. *The New Peoplemaking*. Mountain View. California: Science and Behavior Books, 1988.

Seligman, M.E. *What You Can Change, and What You Can't*. New York: A.A.Knopf, 1993.

Serber, M. Book review of *Your Perfect Right*. *Behavior Therapy*, 1971, 2 253-254.

Seville Statement on Violence, *American Psychologist*, October 1990, pp. 847-848.

Shapiro, F. and Forrest, M. S. *EMDR: Eye Movement Desensitization and Reprocessing*. New York, Basic Books, 1998.

Solomon, R. *About Love*. New York: Simon and Schuster, 1988.

Tanabe-Endsley, P. *Project Write*. El Cerrito, California: Author, 1974, 1979. (1421 Arlington, 94530)

Tannen, D. *You Just Don't Understand*. New York: Ballantine, 1991.

Tavris, C. *Anger: The Misunderstood Emotion*. New York: Simon & Schuster, 1989.

Whitsett, G. *Guerrilla Kindness*. San Luis Obispo, California: Impact Publishers, Inc. 1993 (now out of print, but available in many libraries).

Williams, R. and Williams, V. *Anger Kills*. New York: Times Books, 1993.

Wolfe, J. and Fodor, I.G. A cognitive-behavioral approach to modifying assertive behavior in women. *The Counseling Psychologist*, 1975, 5 45-52.

Wolpe, J. *The Practice of Behavior Therapy* (fourth edition). New York: Allyn & Bacon, 1992

ONLINE RESOURCES OF INTEREST

There are thousands of self-help resources online, and it can be tough to sort the wheat from the chaff. The short list offered here includes sites we consider of value because they meet the following criteria: (1) they are addressed to a general audience; (2) they are produced by qualified professionals; (3) they offer helpful information directly; (4) they offer links to other potentially useful sites; (5) they are not primarily designed to sell products. Web sites change very quickly, of course, and this list may no longer be up to date by the time you are reading it. When you're seeking information or help on the Web, we urge you to use caution, and to apply these same criteria.

Self-Help Magazine: www.shpm.com Psychologist Dr. Marlene Maheu conducts an online magazine with a wide range of moderated self-help resources.

Mental Help Net: www.mentalhelp.net Another easy-to-use accessway to mental health topics on the Internet. Organized into sections: Disorders & Treatments; Professional Resources; The Reading Room; Community

PsychCentral: www.psychcentral.com Psychologist Dr. John Grohol is a pioneer in online psychology and has put together arguably the most comprehensive collection of online resources – both direct information and links available on the Web.

Social Anxiety Institute www.socialanxietyinstitute.org The Social Anxiety Institute is specifically aimed at helping individuals who are highly fearful in social situations. If you found yourself wanting more from chapter 10, this is the Web site for you.

The Infinite Mind: www.infinitemind.com This site centers on the National Public Radio program, *The Infinite Mind,* hosted by psychiatrist Dr. Fred Goodwin. Among topics of interest on recent programs: Happiness, Anxiety, Shyness, Cyberpsych, Courage . . .

Finally, Dr. John Grohol, whose "psychcentral.com" site is noted above, has also authored a comprehensive print guide to Internet sites: *The Insider's Guide to Mental Health Resources Online.* The book has been updated annually, and is published by Guilford Publications in New York.

Index